If you sense God ha
Jesus Christ to anoth
Pursuing the Call. F
El Salvador to prov
principles to get to ti. ...., ... common challenges,
and stay healthy for a lifetime of effective service.

MW01290862

Alan Ehler
**Dean, Southeastern University's Barnett College of Ministry
and Theology**

I have known Danny Lamastra for a number of years and have observed his journey in discovering, developing, and deploying his calling to missions. His passionate heart, prepared mind, and engaged hands are obvious in this book as he shares valuable information and experiences from his recent assignment to El Salvador. *Pursuing the Call* is a must-read for anyone preparing to enter the mission field but also a wonderful resource for family, friends, and mentors of those in the process of posturing for this great adventure. Enjoy!

Sam Hemby, Ph.D.
Professor of Leadership, Southeastern University

Aspiring missionaries need the insights provided by those who have gone before them, but most missionaries do not share their experiences until they have forgotten many of their early challenges and struggles. Danny has provided unique insights and practical advice gleaned from his challenges while they are still fresh in his mind. He has experienced enough to understand the real challenges missionaries face while still close enough to the beginning to grasp their excitement and idealism.

In *Pursuing the Call* Danny provides advice that is clear, concise, and conceivably implemented. His words will spare new missionaries from many tears and much anguish of the early years on the field and will play a role in assuring that others make it past the daunting, two-year mark. A must-read for anyone seriously considering serving overseas.

Michael Peterson
Co-Founder and President, MissionSake

Pursuing the Call is an opportunity to travel on a journey with a young missionary. It is an opportunity to share the good news of salvation and learn about ourselves and our partners in the ministry. Danny Lamastra has been on this journey and has articulated his experiences and insights that may help others who will answer the call to be a cross-culture communicator of the gospel. This book is very practical and helpful.

Dr. Bob Houlihan
Professor Emeritus, Southeastern University

"Unfair!" That's what I felt after reading Danny's book. It was unfair that I did not have such a book when my wife and I embarked on our missionary journey. We would have avoided many mistakes, been much more prepared, and learned things much quicker. Throughout the book, Danny was thinking of the reader and the things that are extremely helpful to know when starting out in missions. He left no stone unturned. This book will be a blessing to countless numbers and help smooth their transition to wherever the Lord may lead them.

Dave Flynn
Latin America Team Leader, Center for Mission Mobilization

Pursuing the Call is a practical guide for those entering the mission field. Though Danny writes from his own perspective as a U.S. missionary, the concepts and principles he teaches apply to all missionaries, particularly those going to a foreign country. Danny writes candidly, sharing many personal stories that illustrate his points with his own unique sense of humor that is so refreshing. His work is comprehensive, insightful, and a delight to read.

Barbara Rowe
Personnel Director, Christ for the City International

In *Pursuing the Call*, Danny does a tremendous job of sharing personal experiences, practical tips, and scriptural guidance. It is truly a must-read for anyone considering missions.

Todd Spires
Lead Pastor, Arlington Baptist Church

PURSUING

the

CALL

Register This New Book

Benefits of Registering*

- ✓ FREE **replacements** of lost or damaged books
- ✓ FREE **audiobook** – *Pilgrim's Progress,* audiobook edition
- ✓ FREE information about new titles and other **freebies**

www.anekopress.com/new-book-registration

*See our website for requirements and limitations.

PURSUING
the
CALL

A Practical Guide for New and
Prospective Missionaries

DANNY LAMASTRA

ANEKO
PRESS

We love hearing from our readers. Please contact us at www.anekopress.com/questions-comments with any questions, comments, or suggestions.

www.cfci.org/dannylamastra
Pursuing the Call
© 2020 by Danny Lamastra
All rights reserved. Published 2020.

Cover Design: Jonathan Lewis
Editors: Sheila Wilkinson and Ruth Clark

Printed in the United States of America
Aneko Press
www.anekopress.com
Aneko Press, Life Sentence Publishing, and our logos are trademarks of Life Sentence Publishing, Inc.
203 E. Birch Street
P.O. Box 652
Abbotsford, WI 54405

RELIGION / Christian Ministry / Missions
Paperback ISBN: 978-1-62245-694-9
eBook ISBN: 978-1-62245-695-6
10 9 8 7 6 5 4 3 2 1
Available where books are sold

Contents

Introduction

Becoming a missionary is the hardest thing I have ever done. To be honest, I did not expect it to be as hard as it was. I had done everything I could to prepare for the transition. I studied the language; I learned about the culture, and I visited the region. However, when it came time to actually move to a foreign country and begin my ministry assignment, reality hit me like a ton of bricks. There were times in those first few months when I didn't think I was going to make it, and the thought of jumping ship crossed my mind on many occasions. But now, looking back, I am thankful that I decided to stick it out. The experiences I have had, the people I have met, and the lives I hope to impact make it worth all the effort.

I recently passed my two-year anniversary of being a foreign missionary, so my time as a "new" missionary is ending. While this period of mission work is still fresh in my mind, I have decided to write a practical guide for new missionaries and for those who are considering foreign missionary service. I hope I can provide advice for your journey as you discern and pursue God's call. One of my pastors used to say, "You don't have enough bones in your body to learn everything from experience." I hope that the lessons I've learned and recorded here will help you break fewer bones.

There is a Scripture that has helped to shape my journey as a missionary. In Matthew 16, Jesus has the famous conversation with His disciples in which He asks, *"Who do you say I am?"* After Peter affirms his belief that Jesus is the Messiah, Jesus says, *"On this rock I will build my church, and the gates of Hades will not overcome it"* (Matthew 16:18). Many have speculated whether the *rock* is Peter himself or rather the confession made by Peter that Jesus is the Messiah. I happen to think it's a little of both, but I'd also like to suggest a third possibility. Jesus may have also referred to the *rock* in a literal sense, meaning the place where they were present as they had this conversation.

Caesarea Philippi, where this conversation took place, was widely known as a center for pagan worship during Jesus' day. The specific religious practices incorporated into the worship of the region were quite perverse. If you look at pictures of Caesarea Philippi, you will also notice that the region is quite rocky. Given the intentionality with which Jesus operated, He may have intentionally chosen to have this conversation in Caesarea Philippi to communicate to the disciples something about the type of church He was going to build. Namely, Jesus' church would be established in the parts of the world and nooks of society that are farthest from Him, that seem the most hopeless, and that are written off as a lost cause. Establishing this church is the mission to which Jesus was calling the disciples, and it is this same mission to which He continues to call us two thousand years later. I invite you to join me on this journey, and I wish you God's best as you pursue His call.

Chapter 1

My Story

"Dear Jesus, I believe in you. Please forgive me of my sins. I accept you as my Savior. Amen." I prayed this with my parents one Wednesday before going to the weekly boys' ministry at my church. I was six years old. To be honest, I don't remember what I actually said, but it was something like that.

I grew up in a Christian home, and both of my parents were involved in ministry. My mom was the vacation Bible school (VBS) director and worked at my church's Christian school for many years. My dad, a licensed minister, was on the worship team and provided pastoral care and church services at an assisted-living facility. Church was never optional, but it was never forced either. I enjoyed being part of my church, and I enjoyed my family's involvement in ministry.

On a regular basis, itinerant missionaries would visit to preach and receive a special offering. My favorite was Doug Stoll, a missionary to Thailand, because he did magic tricks for the children's ministry. When I was in kindergarten, I did a school project on what I wanted to be when I grew up. I naturally chose to do my project on being a missionary, not knowing that it would one day become a reality. However, I definitely would not consider myself one of those people who always knew what they wanted to be. I had my mailman phase, my journalist phase, my fireman phase, and every other phase you can imagine, just like any other kid. There was even a time when I thought I could never be a missionary because I wouldn't be able to watch my favorite baseball team, the Phillies, play their games on TV. As the years went by, though, I continued to be exposed to the world of missions through my church.

When I entered high school, many changes took place in my life. My church transitioned to a new pastor and youth pastor, I changed schools, and my best friend moved away. My freshman year was rough, because I didn't have many friends. At the start of my sophomore year, a rumor circulated that I could rap, and although I didn't know much rap music, I ran with it because people thought it was cool. I decided to purchase a Christian rap album that my neighbor had shown me, Lecrae's *After the Music Stops*. I fell in love with the music and bought more and more albums.

Even though I enjoyed the musical style, what really blew me away were the lyrics. I can't recall ever having heard music that was so overt in its gospel presentation. What started as something to help me make friends became a tool that discipled me and opened me up to a whole new world. I had grown up in the suburbs and had never spent any real time in what would be considered the inner city. However, song after song continued to speak of the need for urban missionaries to preach the gospel in urban contexts. One of the songs that impacted me most was Lecrae's "Beautiful Feet," based on Romans 10:15, *How beautiful are the feet of those who bring good news!* Every time the song reverberated through my headphones or speakers, it presented me with a challenge to think beyond my immediate context to bigger ways that God might be able to use my life.

At the same time that such songs left their impression on

me, my relationships with my youth pastor and members of the youth group grew, and my faith grew. Every summer we dedicated a week to serving our local community, and those days remain some of my favorite summer memories of my high school years. In the summer between my junior and senior year, my church took a group on a mission trip to Mexico to visit a missionary and volunteer in two vacation Bible schools in Oaxaca. It was my first time out of the country, and I quickly regretted it, as I spent the first two days with stomach sickness and an inability to keep food down. Once that passed, however, the trip became one of the greatest weeks of my life.

I remember particularly a boy named Carlos who came to the VBS. Carlos had a very short attention span, in part because he came from an impoverished family and did not get adequate nutrition at home. The only thing that could captivate Carlos's attention was a soccer ball, but his shoes did not fit properly, and when he kicked the ball, his shoe would fall off. It soon became a game. He would kick the ball to me, and I would help him put his shoe back on before kicking the ball back to him. I couldn't understand much of what he said, as I did not speak Spanish at the time, but the experience left an impression on me long after I returned to the States.

When it came time to choose a college, I decided I wanted to go to a Christian university in case I decided to pursue full-time missions. I chose Southeastern University in Lakeland, Florida, and began my college education in the fall semester of 2011. Once again I found myself in a situation where I knew few people and needed to make friends. I watched for opportunities to meet people with similar interests. I had a desire to find an urban ministry where I could volunteer and explore the interest that the music had exposed to me. Shortly after the semester started, a flyer was distributed to all students advertising the Dream Center of Lakeland, an urban mission center near campus. I seized the opportunity to attend the informational meeting they offered.

To make a long story short, I ended up volunteering at the Dream Center for the remainder of my undergrad program, first in their Adopt-A-Block ministry and then as a coach for three seasons in a basketball league that they hosted for youth in the community. I enjoyed the ministry and made many friends in the process. My time at the Dream Center was one of the greatest aspects of my college experience and arguably the most formative as well. The more I served there, the more I considered going into full-time urban missions. Though my sights were set primarily on urban communities in the United States, my vision was soon to expand.

When I started college, I really did not know what I would choose as a major. I had many interests, and I didn't decide on my major until my third year. From the start, however, I had wanted to minor in Spanish, because I just liked the idea of learning another language. I had no specific aspirations that would require me to speak Spanish, and I doubt I could have located more than three or four Spanish-speaking countries on a map. I now believe God gave me the desire to know another language to prepare me for the path He had for me. I soon realized that it is impossible to learn a language without also studying a culture. As my language studies progressed, I became intrigued by the history and culture of Latin America. My professor made it a priority to incorporate this into the class, and I developed an interest in ministry work in Latin America. This process took a few years, but two moments stand out to me as particularly challenging.

The first came in the summer after my sophomore year when I participated in the university's inaugural study-abroad program in Nicaragua. We traveled to many parts of Nicaragua, and I learned much about the country in the process. One place we visited was the city of Granada, which is situated on the shore of Lake Nicaragua at the base of Volcán Mombacho. Many years ago, a volcanic eruption formed hundreds of tiny islands off the coast of the lake, and today tourists can take boat tours through these islands. As we took such a tour, the economic disparity between the islands astonished me. One island would have a multi-million-dollar vacation home, and another, just a few islands away, would display a humble shack made of sheet metal and miscellaneous scraps.

As we traveled through these islands and I continued to see this phenomenon, I became angry. How could someone with such great wealth live in such close proximity to people in dire poverty and not do something about their neighbor's situation? I don't remember at what point it clicked, but at some point another thought struck me. Although I was not the owner of any of the aforementioned vacation homes, I was extremely wealthy in comparison to the families living in the shacks. I was not less aware of the reality of poverty than any of the vacation homeowners. What was I doing to effect change in the lives of the poor? Perhaps more importantly, now that my eyes were opened, what would I do about the problem of poverty? That thought stayed with me long after the trip.

The second occasion came in the final semester of my undergraduate program. My roommate was in a leadership position in a campus club that started a project in Honduras in partnership with a local ministry. After he visited the ministry for the first time, he encouraged me to go on the next trip. I resisted because the trip was scheduled over spring break, and I didn't want to give up my vacation for this trip. However, he eventually wore me down, and I signed up to go on the trip with him.

When we arrived in Honduras, we connected with a ministry called Compelled by Christ that helped girls who had been victims of childhood sex slavery. I had never been exposed to anything of this magnitude, and I wasn't sure what to expect. What I definitely did not expect was the joy I found on the face of a little girl named Kenia. She had been prostituted by her mother and had a heart-wrenching story. What amazed me about Kenia, though, was that despite the horrific trauma she had lived through, she still was able to smile, laugh, and find joy in life. The transformation that she had experienced in her life through this ministry was much greater than I could have imagined possible. I couldn't help but think that if ministries existed to help facilitate that type of gospel-centered transformation in the lives of marginalized people, I wanted to be a part of them.

When I finished school, I looked for ministry opportunities in Latin America. Although I did not have any particular country or ministry in mind, I eventually settled on urban ministry in a region known as the Northern Triangle, which is comprised of Guatemala, El Salvador, and Honduras. During my search for a ministry, I found Christ For the City International. I spoke with their base director in El Salvador and decided to visit and see the ministry in person. In December 2016, I traveled to El Salvador for the opportunity to see the various ministries that the organization facilitates in the country.

One such ministry was a soccer program in a juvenile detention center that the criminal justice system reserved for convicted MS-13 gang members. I had written a paper about gang ministry in graduate school, but I had never actually served in a gang ministry or even spent time around gang members for that matter. Nor had I ever been involved in prison ministry, except for visiting a basketball player from the Dream Center league on one occasion who had been arrested for a minor drug offense that did not stand up in court. In other words, both gang-related ministry and prison ministry would be another new experience for me.

Salvadoran gangs carry a bad reputation in the United States, and though I knew far less about them than I do now, I had seen the photos of hardened gang members tattooed from head to toe. I carried this perception with me when I arrived at the prison, but once the activities began, I was amazed at how normal the guys seemed. Although they had committed horrific criminal acts in their past, they were respectful during the soccer program. The ministry reminded me of the basketball program in which I had volunteered at the Dream Center. I do not mean to give the impression that the kids in that program or in the surrounding community were involved in criminal activity or gangs. Aside from two minor instances across the entire league, I was never aware of a single player being arrested in the years that I served there. Rather, what struck me is that although the guys in both groups had difficult backgrounds, the group in the prison had a vastly different outcome. Both groups had come disproportionately from broken homes and low-income communities, but the group at the Dream Center did not engage in nearly the level of destructive criminal behavior as this group of inmates.

Whereas the group at the Dream Center had a place that offered them love and acceptance, in the absence of involvement in such a ministry, ~~many of these inmates had simply been looking for love, acceptance, and purpose, and had found it in the wrong places.~~ For some of them, this ministry that was now engaging them in the prison would likely be their last chance to turn their lives around. El Salvador was considered at the time to be the murder capital of the world, and young men were the primary victims of rival gang shootings. Even within the prison, although all of the inmates were from the same gang, murder was common. To reference Jesus' words to Peter, this seemed like a ministry that was right at the front door of the gates of hell.

After I returned home, I applied to become a full-time missionary with Christ For the City. I requested to work in the prison ministry in El Salvador, and in August 2018, I touched down once again in that country, this time to stay. Since then, I have become the director of the prison ministry, which has grown substantially since my initial visit. In addition to the soccer program, we've offered vocational workshops, literacy tutoring, music lessons, and a library. The heart and soul of the ministry, though, is a Bible reading program that we started in 2019. Participants start with a 100-day plan in which they read through the life of Jesus. Once they finish, they progress to other parts of the Bible as well. After reading each day's assigned passage, they are required to respond to reflection questions in a journal, and we meet once a week in small groups to discuss that week's readings. When the groups finish one of the plans, we hold a graduation ceremony that family members are invited to attend. In the first year of this program, nearly 80 inmates completed the life of Jesus reading plan. As of this writing, the prison ministry is largely suspended due to visitation restrictions related to the COVID-19 pandemic, and we are waiting to see what the future holds.

This has been my journey so far. Along the way, I have learned important preparations to make and mistakes to avoid when entering full-time mission work. In the chapters that follow, I hope to share these lessons with you. I still have more to learn, but I hope you will find this guide helpful and practical in your journey.

Chapter 2

Preparing for Mission Work

"What advice would you give someone who is considering missionary service?"

This question came up recently on a video chat I did with a group of high school students in the United States. It is a common question, and I hope to respond to it in this chapter with what I consider to be the most foundational advice for anyone considering missions. First, though, it is necessary to clarify what a missionary is and who qualifies as one.

Normally, we look to the Bible to understand the parameters of a particular Christian ministry role to see how that role was carried out in the early church. If, for example, we want to know what constitutes the role of a pastor, an evangelist, or a deacon, we'd determine how these people functioned in the early church as recorded in the book of Acts and the epistles. However, the term *missionary* never actually appears in the Bible, even though, based on their work, we consider people in the Bible, such as Paul, missionaries. This does not make the term bad or invalid, as it describes a form of ministry that is present in the biblical text. It only makes the term harder to define.

Some argue that all Christians are missionaries, and this

statement is true in that the Great Commission is a command to all Christians; all Christians should be active in making disciples wherever they are. In other words, all Christians should have a missional mindset and lifestyle. However, when we talk about missionaries, we are generally referring to a specific group of people rather than Christians in general. For the purpose of this book, we will define a missionary as someone who engages in outward-focused ministry, one that is focused on sharing the gospel with people who are not Christians and discipling them – usually in a cross-cultural context as his or her primary vocational focus. This is not to say that missionaries cannot have other sources of income, but ministry is the primary focus of a missionary.

In reference to the question of advice for prospective missionaries, I would like to unpack a portion of Scripture that relates directly to this topic. In Matthew 25:14-30 and in Luke 19:11-27, Jesus shares one of His most famous parables that we now know as the parable of the talents or the parable of the ten minas, as He taught about the kingdom of heaven. There are several differences in the rendering of the parable in the two accounts, leading to the two different names for it, but the general storyline and message are the same.

A man who is rich and powerful sets out on a long journey and does not expect to return home for quite some time. Before leaving, he calls together his servants, puts each of them in charge of particular amounts of his money, and expects them to manage it for him in his absence. Upon his return, the man finds that two of the servants have made wise investment decisions and have doubled the money that was entrusted to them. The third servant, however, has merely kept the money in a safe place and has done nothing to increase the account with investments. Jesus' final words regarding this third servant in Matthew 25:28-30 are chilling:

"'So take the bag of gold from him and give it to the one who has the ten bags. For whoever has will be given more, and they will have an abundance. Whoever does not have, even what they have will be taken from them. And throw the worthless servant outside, into the darkness, where there will be weeping and gnashing of teeth.'"

What's interesting about the third servant is that he is not rebuked for his mismanagement of the money but rather for his failure to act at all. He is not like the Prodigal Son, who squandered what was entrusted to him. Rather, he is apathetic, choosing inaction over action. As a result, while the other servants enjoy increased responsibilities and privileges, the third servant loses the opportunity to do bigger and greater things for the master. The lesson here is clear. We must be faithful with what is in our hand before we can expect to have an increased ministry.

Many people have the perception that preparing for the mission field means going to seminary or Bible college and earning a degree in missions. That is what I thought for a long time. Academic preparation is important, but the most important advice for someone who is considering missions is to get involved in ministry now. If you are not faithful in serving within your current context with whatever resources are available, you cannot expect God to expand your territory to a foreign mission assignment. You must first be faithful here and now, wherever you may find yourself.

This is what Jesus means when He says that the one who has will be given more, and the one who does not have will have even that taken away. We must show ourselves faithful with the opportunities that we currently have before we can expect to be given more. If we are not faithful with the ministry opportunities that we already have, any future ministry opportunities that we might have had will dissipate. ~~The greatest mistake we could make in preparing for missions is to make our preparations merely intellectual without experiencing the work of the ministry in the present~~.

Another example of this principle comes from the life of the apostle Paul, the most famous missionary in the Bible, aside from Jesus Himself. In Acts 9, we read of Paul's remarkable conversion experience. The text makes it evident that God had placed a call on Paul's life that would include foreign missions. In verse 15, we read, *"This man is my chosen instrument to proclaim my name to the Gentiles and their kings and to the people of Israel."*

Much time passes between this event and the onset of Paul's first missionary journey. According to Galatians 1:18, ~~Paul did not return to Jerusalem for three years after his conversion~~. We do not know how much time Paul spent in Jerusalem after returning, but we see in Acts 9:30 that he left the city and returned to his hometown of Tarsus. Later, Barnabas sought Paul at Tarsus and brought him to Antioch, for it was becoming a new hub for the church as many believers fled the persecution in Jerusalem that Paul ironically had helped to spark. In Acts 11:25-30 and Acts 12:25, we learn that Paul spent a year in Antioch before he made his way back to Jerusalem. Only after he returned to Antioch in Acts 13 was he set apart for foreign mission work. Combining the timeline of these events, we can say that probably five years passed between God's initial call for Paul to be a missionary and Paul actually embarking on his first missionary journey.

What was Paul doing during this time? The three years prior to his return to Jerusalem are somewhat of a mystery, since they are only mentioned in Galatians. From that point forward, though, we have a clear picture of how Paul spent his time:

So Saul stayed with them and moved about freely in Jerusalem, speaking boldly in the name of the Lord. He talked and debated with the Hellenistic Jews, but they tried to kill him. (Acts 9:28-29)

So for a whole year Barnabas and Saul met with the church and taught great numbers of people. (Acts 11:26)

The disciples, as each one was able, decided to provide help for the brothers and sisters living in Judea. This they did, sending their gift to the elders by Barnabas and Saul. (Acts 11:29-30)

In other words, Paul began his ministry. He did not wait for further revelation about where to go and what to do. With whatever opportunities came his way in whatever city he was in, he was busy with his ministry. Only after he proved himself did God open the door for him to begin his missionary journeys for which he is so famous today. Some may say that I am creating an artificial distinction by juxtaposing Paul's life immediately before and after his first missionary journey, since he was engaged in the same ministry both before and after, and the only thing that changed was his location. This, however, is precisely the point. Foreign mission work should always be an extension of ministry that you are already doing or have done in your local context.

Many other biblical examples could be mentioned. The Israelites fought battles in the wilderness before they could enter the Promised Land. David fought lions and bears as a shepherd before facing Goliath. Jesus sent the disciples out to do ministry during His lifetime before they assumed church leadership in Acts. As you reflect on this, the principle is clear.

You must be faithful in small things before you can be faithful in bigger things, or as Jesus puts it in Luke 16:10, *"Whoever can be trusted with very little can also be trusted with much."* You must be faithful locally before you can be faithful globally. I can attest to the truth of this. A key factor for me in recognizing God's call to become a missionary to El Salvador was the connection I made between the ministry opportunities there and the ministry I had been a part of at the Dream Center. Had I never been involved at the Dream Center, I could never have made the connection that impacted me during my visit to the prison ministry in El Salvador. Furthermore, I might not have even cultivated enough of an interest in urban ministry to have visited Christ For the City's El Salvador base in the first place. My earlier ministry experience influenced the ministry opportunities I now have and the ministry opportunities I will have in the future. The same will work for you. ~~The precise ministry you choose to volunteer or work in presently should relate to your future ministry goals~~. All ministry is important, and there is a wide variety of ministry that is valid. However, if your reason for serving is partly to prepare for a particular type of future ministry, you should focus on a ministry that relates to that future goal. Working in urban ministry at the Dream Center related directly to my current ministry. Also, prior to moving to El Salvador, I worked for about a year and a half at a Christian nonprofit in an impoverished, predominantly Hispanic community in Philadelphia. Even though my tasks were different in that role from my current responsibilities, it enabled me to improve my Spanish and helped me develop my understanding of poverty.

In other words, if you want to work in youth ministry, you should volunteer in your church's youth group. If you want to work in poverty-alleviation efforts, you should find a ministry that aids low-income families in your community. If you want to go into medical ministry, you should find a Christian medical ministry or a ministry that visits the sick. If you fall in love with the ministry and develop a heart for it, you will know that you are moving in the right direction. If it ends up not being what you had hoped, you can redirect your efforts to a different form of ministry.

~~It is far better to find out now that a particular form of ministry is not a good fit for you,~~ while the stakes are low, than to find out after you've spent years making preparations and fundraising for a long-term, foreign mission assignment and have moved overseas. Also, I am referring here to local ministry involvement where you currently live, not going on a mission trip. Mission trips can be awesome experiences, and you should definitely go on some before committing to full-time foreign mission work. However, ~~a mission trip that lasts one or two weeks cannot substitute for the preparation you will receive in a local ministry week after week, month after month, and year after year~~.

In addition to involvement in a local ministry, ~~try to express your long-term ministry goals to Christian mentors within the ministry and elsewhere~~. This could include the director of the ministry, a pastor, a parent, current or former missionaries, and professors or teachers if you are at a Christian school. Ideally, you want to ~~choose people who have firsthand knowledge of ministry and missions work~~. Many people have inaccurate perceptions of foreign mission work or foreign cultures because they have had little exposure to them. Choose mentors wisely, and once chosen, heed their counsel.

Lastly, academic preparation is also an important tool at your disposal. This does not necessarily mean, though, that you have to complete a degree in missions in order to become a missionary, as I once thought. This common misconception can put some people in a precarious position. They may be far along in their studies and don't want to switch majors. They may have already graduated from college and are not at a stage of life that would allow them to return to school. Allow me to dispel this myth and say clearly that you do not have to have a degree in missions to become a missionary. For example, my bachelor's degree was in organizational leadership.

Depending on where you want to serve, it might even be best you have a degree in a field other than missions, theology, or Christian ministry. ~~Many countries around the world, and particularly those that have the greatest need for a Christian witness, do not grant religious-worker visas to Christian missionaries or allow missionaries to enter the country overtly~~. If your resume only has degrees and work experiences that are overtly related to Christian ministry, it may be more difficult to get into such countries. Even if you go to a country that is open to missionaries, some sort of skill that you can offer is useful. In fact, any degree you have can be used for ministry purposes.

However, formal ministry training is also important, and there are a number of ways to do this. If you are in college or if you are about to enter college, you can choose to do a double major or minor in missions. Some universities offer interdisciplinary degrees that allow you to combine coursework from two different fields, which would allow you to take mission courses as well as courses from another degree track. Both of these options assume, of course, that you are attending a Christian college, which I recommend if you are considering mission work. Even if you major in a field that is not directly related to Christian ministry, the courses at a Christian college or university will incorporate a biblical worldview that can help you understand how to apply the knowledge you're gaining in a ministry context.

If you have already graduated from college, you could consider correspondence courses with a seminary or begin a master's degree program in a field related to Christian ministry. Some churches even have schools of theology or schools of missions in which congregants can enroll. ~~It is important to note, though, that while you may learn some great information in such programs, if they are not accredited, they may not carry much weight on your resume when you apply to mission organizations.~~ Anything that you can do informally to learn more about missions in addition to your formal studies will help as well. That could mean reading books on the subject, watching relevant documentaries, or attending conferences. You can choose from many different avenues. What is important is that you do something to prepare now for the journey that lies ahead.

Conclusion

You can take many steps to prepare for foreign mission work, and each will provide important tools in your metaphorical toolbox. Nothing is more important, though, than personal involvement in ministry wherever you are. Formal training programs serve an important purpose, but no program, degree, or certification can replace the need to be faithful in local ministry before you pursue global ministry. Remember, if you are faithful in seemingly small things, you will eventually have the opportunity to be faithful in bigger things.

Chapter 3

Choosing a Mission Organization

Choosing a mission organization was a difficult task for me. I remember sitting down at the computer and pulling up research I had compiled on the organizations I was considering. I had found roughly a hundred mission organizations that worked in Latin America, and this didn't include the ones I had failed to identify or chose not to include on my list. How could I possibly narrow this down to one organization or mission agency?

I could never have imagined how daunting this task would be with so many mission organizations in existence. Many people who go into missions expect to go through their denominational mission department, but this is not always the best option. Some people belong to nondenominational churches. Others belong to denominations with small mission departments or with no openings for new missionaries. In my case, my denomination had a thriving mission department that was respected internationally, but they didn't have any openings available for new missionaries that seemed like a good fit for me. Whatever the case may be for you, I would encourage you to explore several mission organizations before making a final decision. Even if you think you already know which you're going to choose, it never hurts to research other ministries. You may find an opportunity you had not considered that is a better fit. Many organizations carry on great ministries around the world, so trying to sort through them can feel overwhelming. I suggest ten questions to investigate and determine which mission organization best fits your goals, vision, and abilities. I asked some of these questions during my selection process, but others are questions that I have since come to see as important for new missionaries. Many more questions could be added, and you may have others that are important to you, which I have not listed here. In my opinion, though, these ten are the most important ones to include in your search.

1. Where will the funding come from?

This question has many facets and may not seem spiritual, but it is an important question to ask. Will you be required to raise your own support, or does the agency pay missionaries through a central fund? When I first considered mission organizations, I hoped to find one that did not require missionaries to do their own fundraising. If you are like me in this, I'm sorry to break the news to you that it is rare to find organizations that do not require fundraising. In my experience, the vast majority of mission organizations require missionaries to raise their support funds. There are pros and cons to this model to consider.

One advantage of raising support is developing a personal relationship with your supporters. Whereas missionaries in centrally funded organizations may not know the people that are giving, missionaries that raise their own support get to know every donor. This can help ensure your support is sustained over the long haul. When people know you, they are more likely to be faithful in their giving. During the months that I researched mission organizations, a large and well-known one with a central funding model that I had considered had to unexpectedly bring a large number of missionaries back to the States from their foreign ministries because they did not have enough money in their denominational mission fund to continue paying everyone's salary. This made me reconsider my desire to limit my search to the mission organizations that had a central funding model.

A second advantage to raising your own support is that it forces you to build ministry partnerships. In the New Testament, we see the personal commission of Paul (still going by "Saul") and Barnabas when they began their first missionary journey:

> *While they were worshiping the Lord and fasting,*
> *the Holy Spirit said, "Set apart for me Barnabas*
> *and Saul for the work to which I have called them."*
> *So after they had fasted and prayed, they placed*
> *their hands on them and sent them off. The two of*
> *them, sent on their way by the Holy Spirit, went*
> *down to Seleucia and sailed from there to Cyprus.*
> (Acts 13:2-4)

Ultimately, the Holy Spirit is the one who sends us, but there is also validity in having sending churches and ministry partnerships. This dichotomy is evident in the commission of Paul and Barnabas, where the text says that they were *sent on their way by the Holy Spirit* but also that they were sent by the church in Antioch. Modern missionaries also need ministry partnerships. This can include people that are praying and fasting for you, mentoring and discipling you, supporting you emotionally or financially, and helping you network with other missionaries and ministries

When missionaries raise their own financial support, they develop a broad range of ministry partnerships in the process.

Missionaries who do not raise their own support may have the backing of their home church and Christian friends, but they are less likely to expand their network beyond this. That means fewer people praying for you, fewer people checking in on you, and fewer people that you can turn to when you have a need. I can say from personal experience that I have several ministry partnerships today that would never have transpired if I had not been forced to raise my own financial support.

The third advantage to requiring missionaries to raise their own support is that it allows a mission organization to accept all applicants who qualify to serve a positive role in their ministries without considering whether there is enough room in the budget to pay them. Mission organizations that use a central funding model must always consider the budget; this means there will be times when they turn down candidates who could have made positive contributions to their ministries because there simply were no available funds to bring on an additional missionary.

The self-fundraising model does have disadvantages, however. The most obvious drawback is that it will take you longer to begin your mission work overseas. This is the most common complaint that missionaries have, and I think it is a valid concern. Beyond being an inconvenience, this delay can also make it more difficult for mission organizations to fill urgent needs. A particular ministry may be in need of additional assistance right now or have recently lost a missionary due to an unforeseen reason but not be able to fill that need until someone is able to raise their support.

The second disadvantage of the self-fundraising model is that missionaries may be tempted to make ministry decisions based on what will bring in the most donations rather than on where the Holy Spirit leads them. For example, if a missionary is in a region of the world that has many churches but high levels of poverty, he or she may conclude that time would be better spent in community development projects with existing churches than in church planting. However, a supporting church that could contribute a significant monthly donation might require its mission committee to select only missionaries involved in church planting. The missionary may be tempted to stray from the form of ministry that he or she has prayerfully concluded is the best option in order to engage in a ministry that is more financially advantageous. This example may seem extreme, but when you know your income is dependent upon such donations, it can be hard not to consider how ministry decisions will affect your financial support. This can become unhealthy for the original goal of the missionary.

The third disadvantage of the self-fundraising model is that it has the potential to result in funding disparities according to how successful each missionary is at fundraising. One missionary who is more skilled in fundraising may end up with a surplus while another missionary that is less skilled in fundraising has a deficit. You may think that the one with plenty should give some of their funds to the one in need. After all, God is the Provider, and all the ministries along with their funds belong to Him. Missionaries are people, though, and they have the same human nature that would cause one to want to keep control of the funds they have worked hard to raise. Also, since missionaries likely never see the accounts of other missionaries or other ministries within the organization, they may not even be aware of the needs that others have.

When you spend years developing a support base, there is a tendency to guard those funds for your own support or for ministry projects that you are directly involved in. After all, if you give away funds and then unexpectedly lose a few donors at some point, which is inevitable, you could be in a position where you are underfunded, and most mission organizations do not offer any type of safety net for missionaries who lose donors. ~~In my experience, the standard practice among mission organizations that use the self-fundraising model is that if you don't receive enough donations to your support account to pay your salary, you don't receive your full salary.~~

A final disadvantage of the self-fundraising model is that some missionaries working within this model have felt under-utilized by their organizations. When a ministry has to assume the financial burden of hiring a new missionary, they will be forced to evaluate the cost and benefit of adding that person to their team. Theoretically, they would only hire the missionary if they had a clear role for the person to fill that justified the added cost. They will also have a financial incentive to monitor the missionary's activity to ensure that their investment is being spent well. In contrast, a mission organization that requires missionaries to raise funds may be quicker to approve new applicants without having a concrete role for them to fill. Since it will not cost the organization anything to bring the person on their team, there is no financial reason for them to turn down any applicant that is qualified and has a heart to serve. This has advantages, but it can also result in approving missionaries without adequately thinking through the role they will play in the ministry. As a result, some missionaries may feel that they are not receiving sufficient direction from their organization once they get to the mission field.

More advantages and disadvantages could be cited regarding the self-fundraising model that many mission organizations use, but these are the most prominent in my opinion, and should serve to help you determine which model to prioritize in your personal search. There is no right or wrong decision, but knowledge of the pros and cons of each model will help you to make an informed decision.

Assuming that your organization requires you to raise your

own support funds, your next question needs to be what percentage of the funds you raise will be retained by the organization to cover administrative expenses. All mission organizations of which I am aware will take a percentage of donations for this purpose, but the exact percentage that is applied varies greatly. The percentage tends to be based on the economic reality of the number of missionaries and the cost of the administrative functions. This usually means that ~~smaller organizations~~ use a higher percentage than larger organizations because they have fewer accounts to draw from. This is not to say you should ignore small organizations in your search, but ~~you will want to have a strong enough conviction about the organization's operations in other areas to be worth sacrificing a higher percentage of donations~~.

You will also want to know if you will be required to set your own support budget, or if the organization will provide one for you. Before I researched mission organizations, I assumed they would provide a budget, but I have since learned that this is not always the case. Some will ask missionaries to create their own budget and submit it for approval.

I am a strong advocate of having the organization set the budget for missionaries for several reasons. First, most missionaries have little idea of what the cost of living will be in the country to which they are moving. Second, some missionaries will feel guilty setting what seems to them a high budget and will decide to ask for less than what they actually need. Conversely, if someone sets their own salary, there is always the temptation to set a budget that is higher than necessary in order to make more money. For this reason, I believe it is best that the organization establishes the budget. If you are required to establish your own budget, though, I would highly recommend expatistan.com to see the cost-of-living difference between your current location and where you will be moving.

2. What health insurance coverage is provided?

Mission organizations can use four different models of health insurance:

- A group healthcare plan that all missionaries participate in

- A local group plan in each country which services missionaries in that particular country

- A personal healthcare plan chosen by the missionary who provides proof of insurance annually

- A freedom for the missionaries to choose whether they want health insurance at all

I prefer either of the first two models, which share many of the same advantages. Group plans bring the cost down for participants, and trying to find one's own health insurance plan for use in a foreign country can be a stressful and confusing process for new missionaries.

Whether a worldwide international health insurance plan or a local health insurance plan is best is a matter of preference. International expat[1] health insurance plans will provide the broadest coverage options and generally do not have a network but will instead allow you to go to any doctor. Such plans also give you the option to receive coverage in your home country. These plans will generally have a component for repatriation in the event of a medical emergency, which, though rarely used, is a great benefit if needed.

The biggest drawback of an expat health insurance plan is that it will be more expensive than a local plan, particularly if you are in a developing country. Local doctors will not have payment arrangements with any expat plans, so you will initially pay out of pocket and submit a claim for reimbursement

---

1   *Expat* means "expatriate" or "a person who lives outside their own country."

later, which could take months to be approved, depending on the insurance carrier. Some insurance plans will require the doctor to fill out forms that must be submitted with the claim, and these forms are not always available in the local language. If the doctor does not speak English, you may need to translate. You should always notify the doctor ahead of time if you will need forms completed to assure that he or she is willing to do the extra work.

In conclusion, expat health insurance plans will provide broader coverage options but will be more expensive and less convenient to use. Some local plans in your destination country may also provide a level of worldwide coverage, but there will likely be more limitations when using it in your home country than with an insurance plan specifically designed for expats. Even if your organization does not require you to have health insurance, you should definitely purchase a policy. Not having health insurance as a missionary is an unnecessary risk that could cut years off your ministry when you contract an illness or condition, as everyone inevitably will at some point.

3. What are the organization's retirement policies?

I have heard some missionaries disregard the importance of saving for retirement because they believe it shows a lack of faith in God's provision. I disagree, and a brief examination of the book of Proverbs will find a plethora of verses encouraging wise financial stewardship. Proverbs 21:20 is one of the clearest about saving for the future: *The wise **store up** choice food and olive oil, but fools gulp theirs down* (emphasis added). People are often forced into retirement due to health problems that prevent them from maintaining the same rigor of work as before. This can happen to a missionary just as easily as to any worker, so a wise practice is to prepare financially for this moment and the season that follows. A missionary can raise funds for retirement savings easier than a retired missionary can raise financial support while not in full-time ministry. Failure to have a retirement plan is poor financial stewardship. Where I do find merit in the anti-retirement sentiment is that mission work is not merely a job but also a ministry. All Christians are called to make disciples, from which no one ever retires. In this sense, missionaries never retire from ministry. However, they will likely have to retire from their vocational ministry role. Even if you are able to continue in ministry until your death, having a retirement plan is beneficial because all donations can go directly to ministry expenses when you reach an age that allows you to withdraw your personal support from a retirement plan. If you do not use your entire retirement plan, you can have in your will to leave all or a portion of what remains to the ministry. The amount could be exponentially greater than the original donations because of the compound interest that has accrued over the years.

An extra-biblical proverb, not to be confused with Scripture, illustrates this concept.

> There was once a man who lived in a community that was advised to evacuate due to an oncoming hurricane. A police officer stopped at the man's house and encouraged him to leave, but the man said, "God will save me." A few hours later, when the rain started, his house began to flood. The man climbed to his roof, and a rescue boat soon came to take him to safety. The man refused, however, saying to the rescue workers, "God will save me." As the waters continued to rise, the man was forced to begin swimming. A rescue helicopter arrived to save the man, but he refused, again saying, "God will save me." Shortly after the helicopter left, the

man drowned. Upon arriving in heaven, the man asked God, "I put so much faith in you. Why didn't you save me?"

God replied, "I sent you a police officer, a rescue boat, and a rescue helicopter. What more did you want?"

It is foolish to ignore the resources and wise practices that God has made available to us under the banner of putting our faith in Him. God has blessed us with great financial-planning resources; failing to take advantage of them might not show greater faith – it might show a lack of wisdom.

Most mission organizations require their missionaries to have a retirement savings plan of some kind into which they deposit monthly. Some organizations offer an organization-wide retirement plan, while others allow missionaries to have an individual retirement account (IRA) that they manage themselves. In my opinion, the best retirement plan for foreign missionaries is a Roth 403(b). Your organization would have to offer this plan for you to be able to participate, so that information is valuable when researching an organization. Whether or not this specific type of retirement plan is available should not make or break your decision, but the information is important to have.

4. What is the organization's doctrinal statement?
I have waited until now to introduce this question – not because doctrine is less important, but rather because many prospective missionaries fail to consider the former questions when starting their search for a mission organization. In fact, doctrine is one of the most important things to consider when researching a mission organization, because the whole purpose of your

quest is the ministry, which must stay within the confines of the organization's doctrinal statement.

For example, if you are Pentecostal, but the organization states in their doctrinal statement that they believe some or all gifts of the Spirit were exclusively for the early church, you face a dilemma. You will have to compromise your conviction to uphold this belief in your preaching and teaching, or you will deceive the organization and preach and teach from your own point of view.

In nearly all of the questions I present in this chapter, there is room for compromise. However, when it comes to doctrine, I do not recommend that you compromise your theology by choosing a mission organization that has an aspect of their doctrinal statement that you disagree with. There are so many mission organizations available, and you will be able to find one with which you do not have doctrinal disagreements.

This is not to say that you have to be in complete doctrinal agreement with everyone you work with after getting to the mission field. Many minor doctrinal differences do not compromise the legitimacy of a person's Christian faith, and working across denominational lines in joint ministry efforts demonstrates unity across the body of Christ. When it comes to what mission organization you choose, though, unnecessary friction in your personal life and your ministry will result if you choose an organization that differs from your own beliefs, however minor the differences may seem.

5. To what extent are local Christians incorporated into the ministry and given leadership positions?

I believe that the more local Christians are involved in a ministry, the more sustainable the ministry becomes. Local Christians know the culture, speak the language, and have experience working and ministering in the local context. They will be there long after a foreign missionary is gone. The more a ministry incorporates local Christians, the stronger and more sustainable it will be.

In my organization, preference is given to local Christians over foreign missionaries when choosing area directors. When I began, the base in El Salvador was our only one in the world where the director was not from the local country but rather from the United States. If you are a new foreign missionary, your transition may be easier if the person to whom you report is from your native culture, speaks your native language, and has experienced the same culture shock that you will. However, you should still strive for ample involvement of local Christians in the ministry.

6. How well do you connect with your supervisor and those you will work with in your destination country?

When you begin the process of becoming a missionary, most of your contact is with the central home office. However, when you move overseas, this contact shifts as you report to and interact with the leadership that is assigned to your country and your specific ministry. Ideally, you want to have a great relationship with both the home office and the local chain of leadership, but the more important one is the latter. Identify who will oversee you and who you will work alongside and establish relationships with them as soon as possible. If you are joining an established ministry, I recommend visiting the country to see the ministry and meet the ministry team in person before you make your final decision. If personalities don't click well, the transition may be long and miserable as you integrate into overseas ministry. It may be best to choose a different location where the organization works or choose a different organization entirely if you are set on the country you have chosen.

7. What assistance will you receive to get established in your new country?

Any move requires attention to details, but even more so when the move is international. You will need to navigate immigration requirements, language-learning, housing, transportation, and more. Many prospective missionaries expect their organization to play an active role in facilitating this transition, but this is not always the case. Different organizations have different levels of assistance that they provide to missionaries who relocate overseas. Some are very hands-on, while others take a more passive role.

For example, some organizations have a housing complex or dormitory for foreign missionaries. Others will assign a local leader to find and set up a housing arrangement for the missionary ahead of time. Others will leave it in the hands of the missionary to find his or her own apartment or house to rent or buy upon arrival. Similarly, some organizations will be on top of the immigration requirements in your new country and will help you acquire and present all necessary documents. Others will expect you to work with an immigration lawyer on your own to acquire residency. They may recommend a lawyer, but beyond that, they are hands-off except for providing documents that you notify them you will need. You should confirm ahead of time what concrete support you will receive in these and similar areas. You will want to have as much support as possible to get settled in your new country.

One way to gauge the level of assistance you will receive is to ask how many foreign missionaries the organization sends both in general and to your country specifically. If the organization has not sent many missionaries overseas, they may not have well-established systems in place to help facilitate your international move, even though they may have great intentions. If the information is available, it may also be helpful to find out the average length of stay the organization's foreign missionaries have before coming off the field. If foreign missionaries aren't staying long, it may be an indication that the organization does not support their missionaries well.

8. What types of ministries does the organization operate?

The number of ways to minister is limitless, but no organization can do everything. As a result, many specialize in certain types of ministries but don't attempt to facilitate all of them. For example, my organization does not do church planting. If they ever choose to enter an unevangelized area with few or no churches, this may change, but as long as we are in the proximity of local churches, our model is to partner with existing churches rather than start new ones. If you are passionate about planting churches, we would therefore not be a good organization for you.

The specific ministry mix will change from organization to organization, so you will want to research those that offer the ministries you want. You do not want to go somewhere that you will be doing work you're not passionate about, and neither do you want to be the one to pioneer a new ministry when you are brand new as a missionary.

9. What is the organization's furlough policy?

Most missionaries will need to come back to their home country periodically throughout their ministry in order to renew legal documents, visit donors, raise additional funds, and prevent burnout. Organizations generally call this time *furlough*, *home assignment*, or *itineration*, and every organization manages this differently.

Some have set timelines established; they may require that

missionaries spend a year on furlough after every four years of ministry in a foreign field. Others have more furloughs that are frequent and shorter, and some leave it up to the missionary. To a certain extent, frequency and length of furloughs are matters of preference.

Some missionaries resist furloughs because they don't want to interrupt their ministry, but this can lead to burnout. Missionaries often work in dysfunctional, draining environments, and an opportunity to unplug from time to time can help maintain one's mental and emotional health for the long haul. Even if you don't think you need to take a furlough for this reason, doing so can still be an important aspect of maintaining current support or raising additional support.

10. Do you know anyone with personal knowledge of this organization?

Ministry is always based on relationships, and if you know someone who can speak to the integrity of an organization, their input can be valuable to your decision. I ruled out some organizations during my search based on information from people whose opinions I trusted. When I chose the organization I am with now, I did not know many people with a direct relationship with it, but all of the feedback that I received was positive. Feedback on every organization you are considering from trusted individuals will give beneficial insight. Any organization can look great online or in a brief visit, so vetting the ministry through your existing ministerial relationships can help you choose the best organization possible.

Conclusion

These ten questions about mission organizations will help you research and choose one to be your sending organization. One final question, though, is more important than all of them – where is God leading you? A thorough investigation of mission organizations with the questions here should not circumvent the prompting of the Holy Spirit. An organization may meet all of your requirements but not be right for you if God is not calling you there. Conversely, an organization may fail to satisfy your preferences in some of these areas, but if that is where God is leading you, there is no better organization that you could choose. Let God lead and guide you in your search and decision-making process. After all, it is His call you are following by going into ministry.

Chapter 4

Raising Financial Support

If you have chosen a mission organization that does not require you to raise personal financial support, you can skip this chapter. If, however, you are like the vast majority of missionaries who raise their own support, this is an important chapter, so read on. Raising financial support can be a daunting task for anybody. Some missionaries who are ready to commit to dangerous assignments are scared to call their friends to ask for financial support. While this may seem ironic, it is often close to reality.

My perspective on effective fundraising strategies has changed from when I started this process. For the first several months, I made no progress. I put a lot of time and energy into fundraising but saw very little results. After failing enough times, I learned from my missteps and received support pledges at a much higher rate.

The change was drastic. From June 2017 to March 2018, nearly nine months into my efforts, I had raised less than 40 percent of my monthly support budget. By the middle of June 2018, just three months later, I was fully funded and on a plane to language school.

While a number of factors contributed to this, including working fewer hours at my job to dedicate more time to raising support, my support-raising strategy also shifted in the winter of 2018. The book *The God Ask*, by Steve Shadrach, was one of the biggest influences that changed my direction for raising support, and I highly recommend it for anyone raising funds for missionary service. Also, there is no doubt that God opened some incredible doors that I could not possibly have imagined over the final months. I literally have hundreds of dollars of monthly support pledges that I never solicited, including from people who simply contacted me because God had put it on their hearts to support me.

As you raise support, you will discover that sometimes God provides support that you did not solicit or expect. This does not mean that 100 percent of your budget will come this way. Rather, you will need to be faithful in doing your part to raise support. Returning to the parable of the talents, notice that although each servant received a certain amount of money for which they had not worked, they were still expected to work in their stewardship of these finances. In the end, only the servants who were diligent and faithful in increasing the money through intentional labor received additional blessings from the master. The servant that simply waited for the master to return while taking no initiative to manage the money is rebuked as both lazy and wicked (Matthew 25:26). Practicing good stewardship in fundraising is important because it is often a reflection of how well we manage other areas of our lives, including the ministries which God has entrusted to us. Jesus says as much in Luke 16:11, *"So if you have not been trustworthy in handling worldly wealth, who will trust you with true riches?"*

One of the biggest hurdles that missionaries face is recognizing the legitimacy of their fundraising efforts. They are often embarrassed to ask for donations and feel like a charity case.

Broaching the topic of need for financial support feels awkward when talking to potential supporters. In one of my first phone calls, I stumbled over my words so much that the person on the other end stopped me and said, "Danny, whatever it is you're gonna say, just say it."

A couple factors helped me to get over this. First, there is a biblical precedent that those who dedicate themselves to full-time ministry should receive financial support for their efforts. In the Old Testament, the Levites received the tithe as compensation for their work in the tent of meeting and later in the temple (Numbers 18:21). In the New Testament, Paul draws a direct line between this model and the right to compensation for full-time ministers in general:

> *Don't you know that those who serve in the temple get their food from the temple, and that those who serve at the altar share in what is offered on the altar? In the same way, the Lord has commanded that those who preach the gospel should receive their living from the gospel.* (1 Corinthians 9:13-14)

Paul again speaks to the legitimacy of people in ministry receiving compensation:

> *The elders who direct the affairs of the church well are worthy of double honor, especially those whose work is preaching and teaching. For Scripture says, "Do not muzzle an ox while it is treading out the grain," and "The worker deserves his wages."* (1 Timothy 5:17-18)

Although Paul begins this passage by talking about honoring elders, he quickly expands that honor to imply a component of financial compensation when he says *the worker deserves his wages.* We also know that Paul received financial support during his ministry. Paul alludes to this in 2 Corinthians 11:7-8:

> *Was it a sin for me to lower myself in order to elevate you by preaching the gospel of God to you free of charge? I robbed other churches* **by receiving support from them** *so as to serve you.* (emphasis added)

He makes a similar reference in Philippians 4:15-16:

> *Moreover, as you Philippians know, in the early days of your acquaintance with the gospel, when I set out from Macedonia, not one church shared with me in the matter of giving and receiving, except you only; for even when I was in Thessalonica,* **you sent me aid more than once when I was in need**. (emphasis added)

Although many people have the impression that Paul was self-funded through his tentmaking trade, this was not always the case. Paul clearly had churches that provided him with financial support.

Even Jesus received financial support during His ministry:

> *After this, Jesus traveled about from one town and village to another, proclaiming the good news of the kingdom of God. The Twelve were with him, and also some women who had been cured of evil spirits and diseases: Mary (called Magdalene) from whom seven demons had come out; Joanna the wife of Chuza, the manager of Herod's household; Susanna;*

*and many others. **These women were helping to
support them out of their own means.*** (Luke 8:1-3,
emphasis added)

Though this passage is not well known, it is obvious that Jesus
accepted financial support.

Lastly, we can learn from Jesus' instructions to the disciples
on how their material needs were to be met when He sent out
the Twelve in Matthew 10 (also recorded in Mark 6) and when
He sent out the seventy-two in Luke 10. Paul appears to be
quoting from these verses in 1 Timothy. The exact wording
of Jesus' instructions differs in these two instances, but the
essence is the same in each:

> *"Do not get any gold or silver or copper to take with
> you in your belts – no bag for the journey or extra
> shirt or sandals or a staff, for the worker is worth his
> keep."* (Matthew 10:9-10)

> *"Do not take a purse or bag or sandals; and do not
> greet anyone on the road. When you enter a house,
> first say, 'Peace to this house.' If someone who pro-
> motes peace is there, your peace will rest on them;
> if not, it will return to you. Stay there, eating and
> drinking whatever they give you, for the worker
> deserves his wages."* (Luke 10:4-7)

Jesus' instructions in both instances were that the disciples
should meet their material needs during these periods of ministry through ongoing support that they were to receive. People
make two objections to these passages being used in support
of fundraising. First, in these examples the disciples were to
receive their support from the same places where they were

going to minister rather than from others who were sending them. While this is true in these instances, this does not delegitimize receiving support from people or churches in order for a missionary to be sent elsewhere, since Paul received support from other churches while ministering in Corinth and from the church in Philippi while ministering in Thessalonica, as previously discussed.

Second, some would say that Jesus' instructions did not mean they should not solicit financial support before venturing out, but that He wanted them to live by faith that God would provide for their needs. That is why He told them in Matthew not to gather gold, silver, or copper before embarking on their journey, and in Luke not to take a purse. Some commentators have noted that the Greek word translated "get" in Matthew 10:9 does not imply that the disciples could not take pre-existing funds, but rather that they could not take the time to acquire additional funds, as modern missionaries tend to do.[2] To this I would say that the heart of Jesus' instructions is that the disciples were not to fear or worry over financial provision and thereby prevent or delay them from their ministry assignments. They needed to trust that God would provide for their needs.

This echoes Jesus' previous teaching in Matthew 6:19-34 and is still true for us today:

"Do not store up for yourselves treasures on earth, where moths and vermin destroy, and where thieves break in and steal. But store up for yourselves treasures in heaven, where moths and vermin do not destroy, and where thieves do not break in and steal. For where your treasure is, there your heart will be also.

---

2   "Matthew 10:9 Commentaries," *Ellicott's Commentary for English Readers. Bible Hub: https://biblehub.com/commentaries/matthew/10-9.htm* (June 25, 2020).

"The eye is the lamp of the body. If your eyes are healthy, your whole body will be full of light. But if your eyes are unhealthy, your whole body will be full of darkness. If then the light within you is darkness, how great is that darkness!

"No one can serve two masters. Either you will hate the one and love the other, or you will be devoted to the one and despise the other. You cannot serve both God and money.

"Therefore I tell you, do not worry about your life, what you will eat or drink; or about your body, what you will wear. Is not life more than food, and the body more than clothes? Look at the birds of the air; they do not sow or reap or store away in barns, and yet your heavenly Father feeds them. Are you not much more valuable than they? Can any one of you by worrying add a single hour to your life?

"And why do you worry about clothes? See how the flowers of the field grow. They do not labor or spin. Yet I tell you that not even Solomon in all his splendor was dressed like one of these. If that is how God clothes the grass of the field, which is here today and tomorrow is thrown into the fire, will he not much more clothe you—you of little faith? So do not worry, saying, 'What shall we eat?' or 'What shall we drink?' or 'What shall we wear?' For the pagans run after all these things, and your heavenly Father knows that you need them. But seek first his kingdom and his righteousness, and all these things will be given to you as well. Therefore do not worry

about tomorrow, for tomorrow will worry about itself. Each day has enough trouble of its own."

We can recognize the principle of Jesus' command without assuming that it is a universal prohibition of soliciting financial support prior to a missionary assignment. I do not believe this is the intention of the passage much in the same way that I do not believe Jesus' instructions to a would-be follower to *"let the dead bury their own dead"* in Matthew 8:22 and Luke 9:60 is a universal prohibition of funerals. Jesus' instructions here are specific to the people He is addressing and serve to highlight the urgency of the situation. If it were wrong to preemptively solicit financial support for future missionary work, why would Paul say this:

> *But now that there is no more place for me to work in these regions, and since I have been longing for many years to visit you, I plan to do so when I go to Spain. I hope to see you while passing through **and to have you assist me on my journey there**, after I have enjoyed your company for a while.* (Romans 15:23-24, emphasis added)

Unfortunately, we know from history that Paul never made it to Spain because he was martyred before then. The point, though, is that Paul is preemptively soliciting personal financial support in this passage; he is fundraising for a foreign mission opportunity that he had not yet embarked on. This is what you will be doing as you raise support for your ministry. We can therefore say that, in light of the aforementioned Scriptures, receiving financial support for your missionary assignment and soliciting such support is a biblically legitimate method of ministry. However, as we raise funds, we must not allow worry over finances to be the driving force of our ministry decisions.

This theology gives your strategy legitimacy and is vitally important for successful fundraising. You cannot develop into an effective fundraiser until you see your efforts as legitimate rather than as begging for charity. One thing that helped me flip the switch from timidity to confidence was hearing the responses of people that I had asked to become supporters. In the beginning, I felt awkward and uncomfortable when I asked people for financial support, but many people amazed me when they expressed genuine gratitude for becoming a ministry partner. They were excited at the opportunity to be part of the ministry I was proposing.

When you approach people to ask for their financial support, you are not merely asking for their money. You are also inviting them to be part of an awesome ministry that God has laid on your heart. This needs to become your mindset, and many people will be inclined to see it that way also. Even if some people are not in a position to give, they are often thankful that you thought of them.

Myths of Fundraising

If you are like me, you probably have a preconceived notion of what fundraising entails, but once you start the process, you will realize that some of your preconceptions do not line up with reality. You may have heard or imagined many myths about fundraising. Here are three such myths.

1. Fundraising means going from church to church and making appeals in Sunday services.

As I shared in chapter 1, when I was growing up, a constant stream of itinerant missionaries came through my church to preach and receive special offerings. Naturally, when I began fundraising, I tried to follow this model. I soon learned that while church services are a component of fundraising, there is much more to effective fundraising than just speaking at church services. Churches can be a great form of support, and church services are helpful for raising large one-time donations, for it is not uncommon to leave with a donation of several hundred dollars or more after speaking at a church. Also, many people will sign up for your newsletter, which could result in more donations in the future.

However, I found that more pledges for monthly support came from one-on-one visits with people I knew than by speaking in church services. As of this writing, about one-third of my pledged monthly support comes from churches, while two-thirds comes from individuals.

Many people assume that it is best to focus on churches because on average they will give larger pledges than individuals will. My average monthly pledge from churches is indeed higher than the average amount of individuals. However, it is not true that churches always give a large amount or that individuals always give a small amount. Some churches give large pledges, some give medium-sized pledges, and some give small pledges. The same can be said of individuals, and my largest monthly donor is in fact a married couple rather than a church. My point is not that you should choose to seek support from individuals rather than churches or vice versa, but that you should seek support from both and not focus exclusively on one over the other.

Also, every church has its own way of supporting missionaries, and some prefer not to interrupt their regular Sunday morning service to have a guest speaker. Some churches also guard their pulpits more closely than others and will not allow someone to preach whom they have not heard before. Of the eleven churches that provide me with ongoing support, I have only spoken at a Sunday service for seven.

Lastly, don't focus your efforts exclusively on big churches and neglect smaller churches. Big churches generally have larger mission budgets, but they also get many more requests for funds. As a result, they are more selective in choosing whom to support. In contrast, small churches may have a small mission budget, but they will generally focus on supporting a handful of missionaries faithfully. Ultimately, a balanced focus on large and small churches is best, and your relationship with a church is more important than the size of a church.

2. Fundraising is something you must do before you can begin your ministry.

Raising support is not a task that you have to get out of the way before you can do ministry. It is in itself a form of ministry that you will engage in. If you recall from chapter 1, I still remember specific missionaries that visited my church when I was a kid.. Hearing them helped open up the world of missions to me and influenced me towards becoming a missionary. As you meet with people and share at churches, you will spur others on to ministry as well. Someone came up to me several months after I had begun fundraising; he had heard me preach at a supporting church, and he told me that after I preached, he felt convicted to be more involved in ministry. He is now in leadership in the church's worship ministry and young adult ministry. This is just one example of how your time spent raising support can be a ministry in and of itself.

Donors are not merely piggy banks who send money your way but are also people who are partnering with you. They are not paying for *your* ministry. Rather, they are a team with you working in ministry. Because of this relationship, you should contact donors regularly to show your appreciation and update them on the ministry. This is often referred to as donor ministry and is just as valid as any other aspect of your ministry. I try to send a newsletter via email every month, put an update on social media every week, and contact at least one donor personally every week. If possible, my goal is for the personal contact to be an actual conversation over the phone or through a video platform like Skype. This practice is good not only to maintain support but also to show donors that you appreciate and value them and see them as a vital part of your collective ministry.

3. Fundraising ends when the budget is reached.

Fundraising never ends as long as you are a missionary. You need to constantly look to expand your base of potential supporters. Inevitably, some donors will have to change or terminate their support pledges for various reasons. When this happens, you will need to generate new supporters who can fill the gap.

Also, as your ministry grows, you will need funds for new ministry projects. You never want to say, "I would love to pursue this opportunity but don't have enough funds for it." Vision should drive budget, not the other way around. If you believe God is calling you into a new area, get busy sharing that vision and raise whatever support you need to carry it out. When this happens, you will be glad to have maintained strong relationships with potential donors who can help meet this new need.

Tips for Effective Fundraising

I had a drastic shift in my philosophy and strategy for fundraising after spinning my wheels unsuccessfully in the first months of raising support. Once I made this shift, I experienced greater success in my efforts. I learned some tips along the way that I hope will help you hit the ground running.

1. Use your existing network of relationships.

When I started raising support, the idea of going to people I knew and asking them for money was terrifying. I preferred to contact anonymous sources because I didn't have to worry about the potential relationship repercussions of receiving a negative response. The problem, though, is that cold calls or blast emails rarely yield results. If you make enough calls and send enough emails, you will eventually get some responses, but overall you will do a lot of work with very little fruit to show for it.

A more effective way of fundraising is to make a list of every person you know and every church you have a relationship with that may be interested in hearing about the ministry you are pursuing. Notice I did not say, "who you think may be interested in giving," but rather "who may be interested in hearing about the ministry." If you try to predetermine those you think will or won't give and only contact the former, you will inevitably leave people off the list who could have been a great help to you.

Also, your list should not be limited to people currently in your life but also to people you have known over the years, such as college professors, high school teachers, coaches, former mentors, or your Sunday school teachers. Include anyone that you can find a way to contact on the list. Contacting people out of the blue after years of silence to ask for financial support may make you uncomfortable, but these people were often the most excited to hear from me and were flattered that I would think of them as a possible ministry partner after so many years.

Once you have your list, contact everyone individually to set up meetings. Do not give up if you do not get an immediate response, but give it some time and try different forms of contact. Some people are not as attentive to email, text messages, or whatever form of communication you originally used, and others may have simply forgotten to respond. Don't write them off after just one attempt. If you do this, you will run out of contacts long before you have raised your support. However, after several unsuccessful attempts to contact someone, you can cross them off the list.

2. Host a launch Sunday at your home church.

Your home church will be a key partner in sending you as a missionary to your destination. Many people on your list of potential supporters may be congregants at the church, so if your church will allow it, set up a Sunday to publicly launch your support-raising journey. Most pastors are excited when someone from their congregation decides to go into mission work, and they want to make sure the rest of the church is aware. A launch Sunday could include you preaching and the congregation praying over you. You could set up a table after the service to meet with people and share your mission endeavors. Your pastor will decide what the best format is, but most pastors are open to some form of this idea. If your pastor is resistant to the idea, you should try to explain that other potential supporters from your church may reconsider supporting you if the church doesn't seem to want to.

3. Meet with people individually and in person.

There is the temptation to contact people in groups because it saves time and appears more efficient. However, group meetings are not as effective for raising financial support because everyone assumes that someone else in the group will donate. If everyone thinks like this, you may walk out with no new support at all. The larger the group, the more this holds true.

Your goal should be to set up individual meetings with the person or the married couple from whom you wish to ask support. As much as possible, these meetings should be in person.

If someone on your list lives far away from you, you may not be able to meet in person, but you can still try to meet in the most personable way possible. A video chat is the first option, followed by a phone call. If several contacts live far away but are in the same area, a trip with scheduled in-person meetings might be best. Coordination of such meetings is complicated, but they will yield better results.

Also, whenever you set up a meeting, be sure to mention that you are raising support to become a missionary. You don't want to ask them to donate before you've shared your ministry, as this would defeat the purpose of the meeting, but you need to mention something about raising support so the person is not blindsided when you meet. Most people want you to be up-front with them rather than leading them to think you just want to sit down for coffee and catch up, only to find out that you are looking for financial support. Also, if the person has an idea of what is coming, you will have more confidence to broach the topic once you meet.

4. Have an established presentation that you use in your meetings.

When I say to have an established presentation, I don't mean you have to break out a PowerPoint and give a classroom- or boardroom-style presentation in every meeting. You can simply have a conversation, but you need to have a clear idea of what you want to say and in what order. An effective presentation will have three basic parts:

- What led you to feel called into mission work
- What mission opportunity you are pursuing
- How the person can partner with you in that endeavor

If the person leaves the meeting without being able to articulate these three points, you did not make an effective presentation. While the general content of your presentation should remain similar for all of your meetings, you will need to adapt according to the setting. There are some key differences between sharing at a church service and sharing in a one-on-one meeting. When you meet with someone individually, you have full control over what you say and how you present your ministry. In a church service, though, you must submit to any guidelines that the pastor gives you. Some churches do not want the missionary to mention the need for financial support; they would rather allow the pastor to make that appeal on behalf of the missionary. Churches may also expect the missionary to dress a certain way and submit to time constraints during their presentation.

When sharing at a church, you should always clarify expectations with the lead pastor beforehand. Whether you like the guidelines or not, you must submit to them. To neglect the guidelines of a church is poor fundraising strategy, and such public disregard for the spiritual authority of the church leadership that has invited you as a guest is ungodly. That pastor is the one God has entrusted with the church's liturgy and norms, not you.

If you are allotted the time slot of a full sermon to present, don't spend the whole time talking about the details of your intended country and ministry. A missionary couple that was finishing their initial fundraising efforts as I was starting gave me this advice. A brief overview of where you are going and what you are doing is sufficient, but those listening do not need an in-depth history or culture lesson. You may be passionate about this, and you should be, since you are going there. Your listeners, however, will not care as much about this, nor do they need to, since God has not called them to the country in question.

If you are given the opportunity to be a guest speaker in a church service, briefly present your ministry, but then use the remainder of the service to preach on a passage of Scripture that has impacted your life, ideally one that is related to missions. People come to the church service to hear from the Word of God, not just to hear about you. Remember, fundraising is not merely about raising funds for a future ministry, but it is also a ministry opportunity in and of itself. If the congregation sees that you can present the gospel effectively and with conviction throughout your sermon, they will be more likely to contribute their support than if you share rote information about where you are going.

5. Reserve a gathering place after every church service when you speak.

I continue to convey here that it is always best to interact with people in the most personal way possible as you raise support. When you present at a church, a move from the large-group context to small group or even one-on-one contact is always best. To facilitate this, you need a display set up that can serve as a gathering place or meeting point to interact with people after the service. This is not an opportunity to ask for their financial support, as this is usually frowned upon by churches, but it is a chance to meet people, talk with them, and give them the opportunity to sign up for your email newsletter (which should always include a donation link at the end). Ask the pastor beforehand for permission to set up a table in the lobby on which you can display your prayer card, flyers about your ministry, physical photos or a scrolling electronic photo frame, your newsletter sign-up sheet, and anything you can find that is representative of the country where you will minister. I have never had a pastor deny this request.

6. Ask for financial support directly.
Many missionaries are great at sharing their testimony and their plans for the mission field, but when it comes to the point in their presentation in which they need to close by asking the person to become a financial supporter, they fizzle out completely. James 4:2 says, *You do not have, because you do not ask* (ESV). While the context of this verse is quite different from our discussion here, it remains true that if you do not ask for financial support, you will get it less often. This is especially true in the United States, as well as in many other Western cultures, where there is a very direct communication style. If you are in the Northeast or on the West Coast, this is even more true. If you do not ask directly for financial support, many people will assume that you were just excited to tell them about your ministry and will not realize that this is what you are seeking. If you want financial support, you must ask for it. Also, if you are primarily looking for monthly support pledges rather than one-time donations, you need to specify this. If the other person tells you that they need time to think and pray about it, as is often the case, ask when you can contact them again to get their decision; then contact them as planned. Even if the answer ends up being no, you need a definitive answer so you know where you stand in your fundraising.

Of course, this does not apply if you are presenting in a church where the pastor has asked that you not discuss your need for financial support. In this case, you would still ask directly, but your request would be to the pastor or missions committee in private rather than during the service.

7. Continue expanding your network.
Anytime you meet with someone, in addition to asking for their personal financial support, you should also ask if they would

be willing to facilitate a meeting with their church's pastor, missions committee, small group Bible study, or anyone else they think may be interested in hearing about your ministry. Not everyone will be able to do this, but those who are able are usually willing. This expands your network, which you will need to do at some point in your fundraising efforts. I received literally hundreds of dollars in monthly support pledges from this type of secondhand connections.

Another way to expand your network is to ask your pastor and other Christian leaders with respected reputations to write a letter of recommendation for you. You can send this to other churches in your church network or denominational district. Though they do not know you, they will likely know your pastor and be more open to meeting with you than if you cold call or send a blast email. I had multiple churches donate that I never even visited personally simply because I emailed them my pastor's letter of recommendation, and his reputation gave credibility to my request.

8. No meeting is a wasted meeting.

No matter how gifted you are at fundraising, you will inevitably have meetings that you walk out of without any financial support. For quite a while, I allowed myself to ride the emotional rollercoaster of feeling great whenever a meeting resulted in a donation or support pledge and feeling down whenever it didn't. I had to learn that no meeting is a wasted meeting. If nothing else, you encouraged someone who may not have been expecting to hear from you and were able to strengthen the relationship. Also, you never know what financial support may result from the meeting in the future.

As an example of this, when I got close to my full budget, I was anxious to finish. I had a meeting with a couple whom I hadn't seen in years but that I thought would be potential supporters. They did not make a support pledge during the meeting or in the weeks that followed. I continued fundraising and assumed that nothing had come of the meeting. Then months later, I received a sizable monthly pledge from a church I had never visited or contacted. It turned out that the couple had taken my information to their church's missions committee and had presented it so strongly on my behalf that the church decided to make a monthly pledge without ever meeting me. The couple also made a monthly pledge later, and both the couple and their church are still monthly supporters today. This taught me that you never know what may come of a meeting, and no meeting is ever a waste of your time.

Regardless of whether a meeting results in a donation or support pledge, you should ask the other person if you may have their email address and add them to your monthly newsletter contact list. This applies even if a person denied your request for a meeting. You may think, "If they didn't even want to meet with me, why would they want to receive my newsletter?" Some people who know they cannot give will deny the meeting because they are embarrassed to have you present to them, only to turn you down afterwards. This doesn't mean that they're not interested in your ministry; it also doesn't mean that they won't become donors later or faithfully pray for your ministry. It is quite rare that someone will object to being included on your monthly newsletter contact list.

The reason it is important to grow your newsletter contact list as large as possible is twofold. First, that newsletter is one of the best ways to let people know how they can pray for you whether they are donors or not, and you, of course, want as many people praying for you as possible. Second, your newsletter list will become your primary contacts for raising additional support in the future. Mass email platforms such as Mailchimp keep stats for all contacts and give each one a rating based on how much they interact with your content. This allows you to see who follows your ministry most closely and who presumably might be the most likely to give if you need to raise funds in the future.

9. Have a dynamic video and print materials.

They say that a picture is worth a thousand words, and if that is true, then a video is worth even more. The majority of the people that you meet with will have never been to your designated country, nor will they ever come to visit you there. In order for them to visualize the ministry, a video that is roughly three to four minutes long will engage them personally. You can present your story and your intended ministry using video clips from that region of the world and that ideally shows the ministry itself. I made a video like this while I was fundraising, and regardless of whether I was speaking at a church or meeting with an individual, I always showed the video at the start of any presentation if the person had not already seen it. I also uploaded it to YouTube and often included the link whenever I contacted someone new through email to request a meeting. The video grabbed people's attention and set the mood for the presentation.

I was fortunate to have a dad who worked for twenty-five years in the television industry, so I had access to a professional studio and all of the equipment I could possibly need to create a great video at no charge. If you do not have this luxury and do not have video-editing skills yourself, I recommend spending money to hire a professional to create a quality video. Most mission organizations can provide you with videos of the ministries, and you may have some videos that you took when you visited the mission, which you should have already done by this time. Any additional clips that you need from the country can be taken from stock footage online or from YouTube videos that are labeled as Creative Commons.

Additionally, three print materials are beneficial to every missionary:

- A missionary profile
- A pledge card
- A prayer card

A number of platforms exist from which you can create these materials if you are tech-savvy, such as Canva or Microsoft Publisher. These need to look professional, though, so pay a professional if you need assistance with the design. You should also pay for a professional printing service after the design is complete. I have included samples of my personal print materials at the end of this chapter to give you an idea of what each might look like and what information they should include.

A missionary profile is a one-page flyer that gives a quick overview of who you are, what your ministry is, and how people can support you. Essentially, it is a condensed version of everything you would include in a presentation if you were meeting with someone. Anytime you have a meeting, you should leave the person with a copy of your missionary profile as a reminder of everything you discussed. You can also send it as a PDF to churches whenever you request a meeting with the pastor or missions committee.

You may think that pledge cards are an outdated tool, as many of your donations will come from online giving. However, some people still prefer to send a physical check to your mission organization, and these donations must be accompanied by a pledge card to indicate which missionary receives it. Your pledge card should give all of the information needed for both online donations and mail-in checks. Some people will return the completed physical pledge card or send it with their donations to your mission organization, and others will set up their pledge electronically. Since some will send the pledge card in the mail, it must fit easily into a standard mailing envelope.

Lastly, a prayer card is probably the most standard print material that missionaries use. Some may argue that a prayer card is just a business card that has been renamed with Christianese, but I disagree. This card should include your contact information and can thus serve some of the same functions as a business card, but the prayer card is indeed distinct from a business card, for its purpose is primarily to remind people to pray for you. It is easy for financial support to become the main thing you focus on as you prepare for the mission field, but prayer support is extremely important. Many people save these cards and pray for the missionaries on them.

Conclusion

You now have the tools you need to raise support for your ministry. Don't get discouraged if it seems like you struggle in this area at first. Most importantly, don't assume that if you struggle to raise support, God is not really calling you to the mission field. Fundraising has a learning curve, but you will get better the more you practice. God will indeed provide you with the support you need if He has called you into ministry, and your conviction of God's call needs to be strong enough to withstand the turbulence of fundraising woes. Bigger challenges than this will lie ahead, but don't be overcome by anxiety, and don't forget to enjoy the experience. This is a unique time in your mission journey, and with an eternal perspective, you will look back on it with fond memories of reconnecting with old friends, forming new partnerships, and watching God provide in amazing ways.

Sample Print Materials

Danny Lamastra

MISSIONARY TO EL SALVADOR

When I began college in 2011, I decided to minor in Spanish with no real consideration of becoming a missionary to Latin America. Over time, though, God began to lay a burden on my heart for this region of the world. Shortly after graduating, I committed to become a missionary to El Salvador with Christ for the City International. El Salvador is the murder capital of the world and serves as the base for transnational gangs MS-13 and 18th Street. During my time there, I plan to minister in juvenile detention centers comprised primarily of convicted gang members.

CFCI.ORG/DANNYLAMASTRA | DANNYLAMASTRA@GMAIL.COM | @DANNYLMISSIONS

Missionary Profile, Front

QUICK FACTS

Up to 1 in every 12 people in El Salvador have ties to a gang.

El Salvador is the murder capital of the world, with one murder every hour and fifteen minutes in 2015.

Christ for the City has eight unique ministries in El Salvador.

HOW YOU CAN SUPPORT ME

1. Pray for our ministry.
2. Send me your email to get my newsletters and video updates.
3. Host me at your home or church to share my vision.
4. Follow me on social media.
5. Give online at www.cfci.org/dannylamastra

No place without a vision, no church without a mission, no person without hope

CFCI.ORG/DANNYLAMASTRA | DANNYLAMASTRA@GMAIL.COM | @DANNYLMISSIONS

Missionary Profile, Back

Pledge Card, Front

Yes, I would like to help fund Danny Lamastra's ministry with CFCI.

Amount:
- ☐ $500 ☐ $250 ☐ $100
- ☐ $50   ☐ $35   ☐ Other_____

Frequency:
- ☐ One Time   ☐ Bi-Weekly   ☐ Monthly
- ☐ Quarterly ☐ Annually   ☐ Other_____

Fund:
- ☐ Support   ☐ Travel & Equipment   ☐ Work Funds

Please call (402) 592-8332 if you would like to set up automatic withdrawals for future donations.

_____
Name

_____
Address

_____
City / State / Zip

_____
Phone Number

_____
Email

Note: Please make all checks payable to Christ for the City. Per IRS regulations, please always include a separate slip saying whose account your donation should go toward rather than writing "Danny Lamastra" on the memo line of checks.

Thank you for your generosity!

Pledge Card, Back

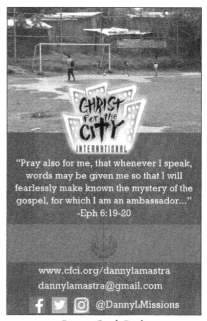

Prayer Card, Front   Prayer Card, Back

Chapter 5

Learning the Language

If I had a dollar for every language blunder I've made since I started learning Spanish, I could have skipped the chapter on fundraising because I'd already be funded from now to eternity. I have countless funny stories of words I misused or mispronounced, as does anyone who has learned a second language. Although not my own, one of my favorite stories is of a missionary I met in Colombia. In his first sermon, he wanted to preach about the Spirit of counsel (el Espíritu de consejo). Instead, he preached the entire sermon about the spirit of the rabbit (el espíritu del conejo). I'm sure the congregation was quite confused at this strange teaching! Mishaps like this are a natural part of learning a language.

Language learning is not a task that is unique to foreign missionaries. Many people choose to learn a second language for a variety of reasons, and in some parts of the world, it is even rare to be monolingual. If you want to do ministry in a foreign country, you will almost certainly need to learn another language. Even if English is commonly understood where you're going, you should take the time to learn the local language if English is not the native language.

Nelson Mandela is attributed with having said, "If you talk to a man in a language he understands, that goes to his head. If you talk to him in his language, that goes to his heart."[3] Missionaries are in the heart business much more than the head business. Even if you are able to get by with English, you will have a greater impact on people's lives and a more enriched experience personally if you take the time to learn the local language.

Different mission organizations have different ways to facilitate language learning. My organization required me to go to a language school in Costa Rica before I could be approved to start my ministry assignment in El Salvador. This model is common for Latin American missionaries, but I don't know if this centralized regional language-school model is common in other parts of the world. If you have the option to choose, though, I would recommend a language school or private tutor in the country in which you will be serving rather than a more centralized school elsewhere.

I had a great time in Costa Rica and enjoyed the opportunity to see some beautiful parts of the world I might never have visited otherwise. However, upon arriving in El Salvador, I discovered Spanish is spoken differently there than in Costa Rica, even though the two countries are geographically close. Also, by going to a language school elsewhere, I went through the challenge of culture shock twice instead of once. Although Costa Rica and El Salvador are close and share a common language, some strong cultural differences exist between them. This is somewhat true for any two countries you wish to compare. Although some countries are more internationally renowned for their language schools than others, there will be schools and language-learning opportunities available wherever you go.

---

3   "Mandela in his own words," CNN, June 26, 2008: *https://edition.cnn.com/2008/WORLD/africa/06/24/mandela.quotes/* (June 28, 2020).

Regardless of how your organization facilitates language study, there is no reason to wait to learn any language that you will need in your foreign ministry assignment. You can take practical steps on your own to learn the language once you know where in the world you will be going. This will enable you to begin ministry faster, speak the language better, and potentially save money, since overseas language schools are not necessarily cheap. Here are some practical tips for learning a new language that I have found to be helpful.

1. Sign up for a local class.

Before I learned Spanish, I thought that learning a second language simply meant learning a new vocabulary. Then, once you have the vocabulary memorized, you can insert the words for their English counterparts and speak fluently. I soon learned that this is not the case. Languages do not merely have different vocabulary but also different grammatical structures. The order of words in a sentence can change, and there may be verb tenses that don't exist in English. These differences can be seen, for example, in an interlinear Bible that translates the text word for word without adjusting the grammatical structure and word order. Such Bibles may be useful for studying a passage in greater depth but are barely readable without another point of reference. Furthermore, some languages have an entirely different alphabet.

Learning these complex aspects of language without formal instruction is quite difficult. Phone apps and computer programs designed for self-learning do not necessarily suffice. They may carry some benefit, but they are unquestionably inferior to in-person instruction. If you are still in school, you can sign up for a language class in the upcoming semester. If you are not in school, you could consider taking an evening class at your local community college. You don't have to work toward a degree, but you can complete as many courses as possible in the language you want to learn. Unless the language in your destination country is particularly obscure, you should be able to find some form of local in-person instruction.

It is worth noting, though, that a class is only as good as the effort you put into it. This is especially true if you are auditing the class or not studying toward a degree, as you will be less motivated to work toward a particular grade. Language courses are designed to give you the tools you need to learn a language, but what you do with those tools depends on you. I know people who minored in a foreign language but are unable to carry on a conversation in that language. Merely going to the class or doing the minimum to earn an *A* will not be enough to learn a language. You will only learn the language if you diligently apply yourself to studying the topics presented in the class on your own time.

2. Study vocabulary.

Although there is more to learning a language than learning vocabulary, vocabulary is still an important component of mastering a language. The vocabulary base of native speakers differs between languages because of the difference in structure, but it has been estimated that people know about fifteen to twenty thousand word families in their first language.[4] While you do not need to learn this many words to begin speaking your second language, if you do not develop a broad vocabulary, you will be limited in topics and depth in your discussions.

The nice thing about vocabulary is that it is easy to study on your own, especially if the language uses the Latin alphabet. Frequency dictionaries are useful for learning vocabulary because they list words in the order of frequency of use rather

---

4   Beth Sagar-Fenton and Lizzy McNeill, "How Many Words Do You Need to Speak a Language?" BBC News, 24 June 2018: *www.bbc.com/ news/world-44569277* (June 29, 2020).

than alphabetically. Using one of these to make flashcards that you can add to and study for about fifteen minutes daily is a great method of vocabulary building. Electronic flashcards on a website such as Flashcard Machine rather than physical flashcards may also be useful.[5] You will eventually collect thousands of them, so the electronic version will make it easier to navigate this many.

3. Spend time with native speakers.
The best way to learn a language is to use it in its natural context. If you have the opportunity to study, volunteer, or take an internship abroad, you will learn the local language where you are forced to use it. If you are unable to do this, you can find people who live nearby who are native speakers of the language you want to learn. For example, I had a Mexican-American friend who met with me periodically to speak Spanish while I was learning the language. I also had roommates from Puerto Rico for a couple of years and took a job in a neighborhood with a large Hispanic population.

You may not be able to do all of this, but if you can find one person who can meet with you once a week to speak the language, the practice will help you greatly. Ideally, this person should be a native speaker, as he or she will speak the most naturally and be able to correct you when you make a mistake. Most people will be happy to do this, because it excites them whenever someone shows a genuine interest in their language and culture.

If you are unable to find native speakers to do this, another person who is learning or has learned the language will also be able to help. However, if you meet with someone who is also learning the language, you will likely mimic each other's mistakes. If the other person doesn't understand you, you won't

---

5   Flashcard Machine: *https://www.flashcardmachine.com/*.

know if it's because you said something wrong or if you are using vocabulary or grammar that the other person has not yet learned.

Regardless of whom you choose to meet with for conversations, the key to these meetings is to stick to the language you are learning for the time you have set and not revert to English. The temptation to do that must be avoided as much as possible if you want to learn the language. You can talk in English later.

4. Read and write in the new language.

In language study, reading and writing generally come quicker than speaking and listening. When you read and write you can ponder the meaning of what is being said or what you want to say. You can pause to look up a word you don't know or go back over a section to ensure that you understood it correctly. None of this is possible in a face-to-face conversation, where you must capture the meaning at whatever pace the other person is talking and form your own words without hesitation. Reading books or articles about your destination country in the local language will help you better understand the country and improve in the language at the same time. Corresponding with a local Christian who is directly or indirectly involved in the same ministry will help you learn and simultaneously give you a friend for when you arrive. These easy and practical ways will help you improve your language skills.

5. Listen to music and watch shows or movies.

I found that media, especially music, is helpful in learning a language. It is a constant part of our lives, and we can use this to our advantage when learning a new language. The key is to find music, shows, or movies that you enjoy listening to or watching. I listened to Spanish music as a way to learn the language, but I ended up enjoying the music and acquiring favorite artists. This is important because the more you enjoy the music, the show, or the movie, the more you will naturally listen and watch without feeling forced.

I have heard it said that content created for children is a good place to start because it will have more basic language than content made for adults. This didn't work for me because content created for children wasn't entertaining as an adult, so it didn't hold my attention. I had to force myself to engage and was constantly zoning out. On the other hand, once I found music or shows that I enjoyed, listening and watching became as natural as listening and watching in English. This way I could constantly consume the language.

Original content in your new language is better for learning than content that was originally created in your native language and later translated. Songs that are translated are rarely as good as those in the original language, since much of the poetic creativity is lost in translation. I find trying to watch my favorite English-based show or movie dubbed into Spanish frustrating rather than helpful since the lips don't match up and the voice clearly is not that of the person speaking. Original content rather than translated content also has the added benefit of helping you understand the culture better and not just the language. Choosing content is a matter of preference, though, and if you enjoy translated content, go for it. Whether your choice is original or translated content, the important thing is to learn the language.

6. Don't be afraid to make mistakes.

Of all the tidbits of advice that could be offered to aid in learning a new language, this might be the most important. No matter how much you study a language, you will never be confident speaking it until you practice, and practicing means that you will make mistakes. You will at times pronounce words so poorly that people won't know what you're trying to say, and at other times you will say things that do not mean what you intend to say. Sometimes mistakes can be quite funny, and if you get frustrated instead of laughing, you will have a miserable time learning a new language.

Also, if you concentrate too much on the grammatical perfection of every word, you will speak so slowly that you will never make it through a sentence. In order to get over the hump from head knowledge to conversational fluency, you simply have to let the language flow and not be self-conscious about the mistakes. The most important thing is to be understood, and if what you want to say doesn't come out perfectly, most people will be happy that you made an effort.

Conclusion

Learning a language can be a challenge and certainly will not happen overnight. However, if you keep working at it and don't give up, you will become fluent in the language you want to learn. Whatever your age or educational background, you can learn another language. Sometimes you will get frustrated that you can't communicate as you want, but your efforts will pay off and enable you to have a greater ministry and experience in your destination country. All of the hard work will be worth it.

Chapter 6

Surviving Culture Shock

I f you ever played sports in high school or college, you know that all athletes dread the first week or two of practice. Coaches focus on rigorous conditioning routines with lots of running and comparatively less time actually playing the sport in question. Athletes commonly refer to this opening week as *hell week*, highlighting how unpleasant this part of the season can be. In addition to getting the team in shape, this intense training weeds out those who do not have enough desire to be on the team to push through the pain. This experience isn't pleasant for anyone, but those who want to be on the team must push through it to get to the more enjoyable experience in the remainder of the season.

Going through culture shock is a lot like this initial training when a new season starts in sports, but to a much greater degree. Whereas a sports practice lasts a few hours, culture shock is a reality 24/7 when you first move to a new country. Also, the grueling portion of a sports season is short lived, thus the term *hell **week***, but culture shock can last for several months.

I intentionally chose the word *surviving* to title this chapter rather than a milder verb such as *adjusting*, *coping*, or *dealing with.* When you go through culture shock, every day can be a struggle, and even the most mundane tasks are challenging. Everything you have ever thought to be true about societal norms has to be relearned. You will be tempted multiple times to pull out and go back home before you make it through this period. Before I moved overseas, I thought I would be resistant to the phenomenon of culture shock. Granted, I expected some level of adjustment, but I did not expect the experience to be too severe. After all, I had done so much to prepare for moving to El Salvador. I had studied the language for years, studied abroad in Central America, and later served as the assistant director for that same study-abroad program. I excelled in multiple classes on cultural studies, roomed with Hispanics in college, and worked in a predominantly Hispanic organization. I played on a Hispanic softball team, went on several mission trips to Latin America, and developed an authentic love for Latin America and Latino culture. I believed I was ready for the new culture.

Even with all of these preparations, I plummeted into culture shock upon arrival in El Salvador. Months into my experience, I would still randomly cry as I was overcome by a cloud of depression. I had moved away from home previously when I went to college and didn't experience anything like the level of difficulty that I did moving overseas. A huge part of me wanted to call it quits and leave the country, but I knew I would have to give up on a dream I had worked towards for years and simultaneously let down the people who had given sacrificially to get me to this point. A person whose opinion I highly respected advised me to stay for a year before deciding whether to leave or not. I'm glad I did. In the sixth month, my mental and emotional state started to improve, and I can now say that I really do love El Salvador.

Some things helped me break through the wall of culture

shock, but it is first important to establish what culture is and what it means to experience culture shock. When many people think of culture, they think about the food, dress, and music that are common within a society. These are certainly aspects of culture, but they are merely surface-level aspects of what culture comprises. Different cultures have different communication styles, different ways of understanding how the individual relates to the community, different ways of relating to authority, different ways of viewing time, different social norms, and a whole host of other differences that are deeply ingrained in how a society functions.

Cultural anthropologist Geert Hofstede has defined culture as "the collective programming of the mind that distinguishes members of one group or category of people from others."[6] Missiologist Sherwood Lingenfelter defines culture more simply as "the sum of the distinctive characteristics of a people's way of life."[7] What is apparent in both of these definitions is that culture encompasses every aspect of the human experience. From an early age, your mind is subjected to cultural influences that shape how you think and act and ultimately result in you growing accustomed to a particular way of life that has shared elements with the rest of your society. When you attempt to change cultures, everything you have been programmed to accept as to how life works by your native culture comes under fire, and you are forced to develop a new framework for understanding the human experience. This sharp internal confrontation is called *culture shock.*

Hofstede defines culture shock as "a state of distress following the transfer of a person to an unfamiliar cultural environment."[8]

6   Geert Hofstede, Gert Jan Hofstede, and Michael Minkov, *Cultures and Organizations: Software of the Mind,* 3rd ed. (New York: McGraw-Hill, 2010), 6.

7   Sherwood G. Lingenfelter, and Marvin K. Mayers, *Ministering Cross-Culturally,* 2nd ed. (Grand Rapids: Baker Academic, 2003), 17.

8   Hofstede, Hofstede, and Minkov, *Cultures and Organizations,* 516.

Expounding upon this definition, he explains in more detail what causes this phenomenon of culture shock:

> Our mental software contains basic values. These values were acquired early in our lives, and they have become so natural as to be unconscious . . . The inexperienced foreigner can make an effort to learn some of the symbols and rituals of the new environment . . . but it is unlikely that he or she can recognize, let alone feel, the underlying values. In a way, the visitor in a foreign culture returns to the mental state of an infant, in which the simplest things must be learned over again. This experience usually leads to feelings of distress, of helplessness, and of hostility toward the new environment. Often one's physical functioning is affected.[9]

In addition to adjusting to cultural differences, one of the challenges you will face if you move to a developing nation is a much higher level of general dysfunction than you see back home. A simple example of this is the chaotic driving in some countries. In El Salvador, street signs are not as common as in the States. Intersections often have no stop signs or traffic lights in any direction, and one-way streets might not be marked. On several occasions, people honked at me and freaked out because I was apparently going the wrong way down a one-way street. I used to send passengers into a panic when I drove through intersections that didn't have a stop sign – without stopping. My question in both situations was always, how am I supposed to magically know when I am expected to stop or when a street is a one-way street if it's not marked? The answer was always that you're just supposed to know, but of course, as a

---

9   Hofstede, Hofstede, and Minkov, *Cultures and Organizations*, 384.

newcomer, this is not possible. This example of dysfunction is only one of many that you may experience when you move to a developing country.

I won't describe all of the cultural dimensions and popular models for understanding culture that have been proposed by culture studies, as this would require a full volume instead of a mere subsection of a chapter. I also won't describe the differences between particular cultures in different regions of the world, as those reading this book will likely be going to different parts of the world. I encourage you, though, to study these topics; some resources regarding this are listed in the Recommended Reading section at the end of this book. The message that I want to convey here, though, is simple. No matter how prepared you think you are, you will experience the angst of culture shock when you move overseas.

Also, even though mission trips are valuable for other reasons, they do little to prepare you for culture shock. You might assume if you have taken mission trips and had a great time, you are sufficiently adapted to the culture to be able to move there without experiencing culture shock. This could not be further from the truth. A mission trip is rarely long enough to get past the honeymoon phase and enter into culture shock. Also, mission trips tend to be done in groups with others from your own culture, some of whom may even be friends with whom you spend the majority of your day. The structure of the trip is designed to give you a positive experience. The fact that you have a known end date in the near future when you will return to the comfort of home prevents you from grappling with the most severe cultural differences. Going on a mission trip for one or two weeks with friends and moving overseas indefinitely by yourself are vastly different experiences.

When culture shock hits, I encourage you to follow the same advice that was given to me. Determine that you will wait at least a year before you let yourself call it quits. You will probably discover that by the end of the first year your mental and emotional state will have improved greatly. For several months on end, it may seem like life will never get better, but you will likely hit a turning point before your first year ends. For me, that turning point didn't come until my sixth month, but once it came, everything started to change from a nightmare to a pretty incredible experience. I discovered eleven tips that helped turn the tide for me. I would encourage you to try them when you are in the thick of culture shock.

1. Take some time away.

I moved to El Salvador in August 2018, and in December I came back to the States for my sister's college graduation and Christmas with my family. I was in a dark place before I left El Salvador because I continued to wrestle with culture shock. Being away for a time with no responsibilities helped me recalibrate and get back to a healthy mental and emotional state.

When I returned to El Salvador, I was in a better state of mind than when I had left. Going back to your home country for a visit may not be realistic, depending on where you are in the world, how many people you have in your family who are serving with you overseas who would need a plane ticket, and the expectations of your mission organization. Even if you are able to go home, it may not be the best option; you will need the discipline to get on your return flight to the country of your mission assignment. Also, leaving too soon without an occasion or event could be seen by your local ministry partners as a rejection of them. If a trip back home is not feasible, you can still take a vacation somewhere in the country – a place where you can get away, relax, and spend time with God. This will help you clear your mind and refocus.

2. Find someone who can serve as a local culture guide.

Even though every aspect of your new culture seems strange to you, it makes perfect sense to someone who has grown up there. Find a local who is willing to accompany you on your journey and explain the way the culture works. For me, a pastor named Joel provided this service. He worked in our prison ministry, and we often carpooled to ministry sites. During our time together, he adopted the role of culture guide even though I had never formally asked him to mentor me in that way. Joel was a huge blessing to me, and we continue to work together in ministry.

As you adjust to your new culture, find someone who can serve this role of a culture guide. It may help if it is someone who has experience interacting with people from your home culture since he or she will best know the differences between the two cultures to highlight. Even if this is not the case, though, anyone who is from the culture can help you develop a better cultural understanding.

3. Get active in ministry.

Some mission organizations are hesitant to give new missionaries much work to do; they are fearful of overwhelming them while they are going through the challenging transition of adjusting to life overseas. While I appreciate this sentiment, when I made an effort to become more involved in ministry, it helped me cope with the culture shock. The idle mind wanders and rarely produces healthy thoughts. If your mind is idle, you drift back into the toxic thoughts of regret over your current situation and your desire to get out. The more you can stay productive, the more you can avoid this problem. Also, being active in ministry serves as a reminder of why you're pushing through the culture shock. You felt the call of God to minister in a foreign land, and your pain has a purpose.

4. Get out of your house.

The worst days in my transition were the days that I stayed home by myself and did nothing. While such a day may sound relaxing, especially if you are an introvert, these days were anything but relaxing. They gave my mind endless time to wander and dwell on those toxic thoughts. If you are single and live alone, as I did, you will find this to be especially true. If you are new to a country, you may fear that your level of fluency in the language is not sufficient to move about freely, and you may have concerns about unwittingly venturing into an unsafe area. These are legitimate concerns, and you should use wisdom and take precautions for your safety. However, anything you can do outside your house will give your mind more to focus on. When you are deep in depression, the only thing you normally want to do is curl up in bed and watch Netflix while eating junk food. Resist this temptation and get out and about. You will feel much better at the end of the day than if you had sulked at home all day.

5. Exercise.

This may seem like an odd recommendation for dealing with culture shock, as there is little apparent relation between physical exercise and becoming further acculturated within a new culture. However, I have found that exercise nearly always helps me recalibrate my mind and emotions to a healthier state.

In truth, this is not merely my own anecdotal experience but also a well-documented phenomenon. Scientists and contributors to *Current Sports Medicine Reports*, Andrea Dunn and Jennifer Jewell, note how far-reaching the benefits of physical activity are for coping with stress, anxiety, and depression, all of which are components of culture shock:

> The most comprehensive recent review about the ability of physical activity to prevent mental disorders . . . based on cross-sectional and prospective epidemiological data are that physical activity can protect against feelings of distress, enhance psychological well-being, protect against symptoms of anxiety and development of anxiety disorders, protect against depressive symptoms and development of major depressive disorder, and delay the effects of dementia and the cognitive decline associated with aging.[10]

Even if you have never been much of an exerciser, you will find it helpful to build the discipline of regular exercise into your daily routine. You do not need to become the next great bodybuilder, but any physical activity you can engage in will help mitigate the stress you feel as you go through culture shock.

6. Make friends with other foreign missionaries.

In El Salvador, we have a missionary fellowship for foreign missionaries in the country. Every November, they sponsor a retreat for anyone in the fellowship, which I found to be especially helpful in my first year. Getting to know other missionaries is a good idea, since it enables you to collaborate in ministry, but it also can help with culture shock if you know other missionaries or people from your home culture. These people will have dealt with culture shock as well and will be able to relate

---

10   Andrea L. Dunn and Jennifer S Jewell, "The Effect of Exercise on Mental Health," *Current Sports Medicine Reports* 9, no. 4, (July-August 2010): 203.

to what you are experiencing. As a result, they can help you adapt to the new culture where you both live.

7. Make local friends.

I cannot overstate the importance of forming friendships with people, especially with locals, as you start your time abroad. This might be the number-one factor that helped me overcome culture shock. Some missionaries have the tendency to surround themselves in a small bubble of their missionary community and never venture into the local culture except when they are doing ministry. On the extreme end of this spectrum, some missionary families have lived abroad for years and still have members who struggle with the local language because they spend all of their time in their own community. Such people may be physically present in the country, but they are hardly integrated in the culture.

The less time you spend in the culture, the less assimilated you will become and the more you will continue to wrestle with the ongoing stress of culture shock. Even if you get past the initial stress and are able to function, if you are not ingrained in the local culture, your experience will be far less enriching. The best way to become ingrained in the culture is to make friends who are locals, people who genuinely enjoy spending time together when you're hanging out just for fun and not doing ministry. Having these types of local friendships will open the door to a plethora of incredible cultural experiences that you will cherish for the rest of your life and that you could never have had on your own.

8. Find things you enjoy about the country.

Regardless of what country you go to, there will be some pretty incredible experiences in that country that you did not have available back home. That country is probably receiving a constant flow of tourists who pay thousands of dollars to visit a place where you are privileged to live. When you're not working, take the time to explore the country and find hobbies that you enjoy.

For me, the two hobbies I have come to enjoy in El Salvador are surfing and exploring waterfalls. I had surfed before coming here, but I had never lived anywhere that provided such a high-quality wave on such a consistent basis. I also had wanted to try cliff jumping but rarely had the opportunity to do so before moving here. El Salvador is a mountainous country, so there are plenty of waterfalls to explore that provide the opportunity for cliff jumping. Your interests may be different from mine, and that's perfectly fine. The point is that you should search for experiences in your new country that you really enjoy. You need to take time for rest and self-care, which also has a biblical precedent. If you find things that you love about your new country, they will endear you to your new living situation and advance you through culture shock.

9. Recognize that you don't have to love everything.
Before I moved abroad, I thought that becoming acculturated meant embracing every aspect of one's new culture. While I was in language school in Costa Rica, my teacher shifted this perspective somewhat when we discussed this topic. He basically said, "You're never going to completely lose your native culture and become fully Latino, and that's okay. The important thing is that you understand the local culture and are able to navigate it." This comment caught me off guard, but I have found it to be true.

Some people have told me that I am the most Salvadoran gringo they know, and I have even had a few Salvadorans tell me that I am more Salvadoran than they are. I always consider this a high compliment, but the reality is that there are still aspects of the culture here that are pet peeves for me. For example, I am a time-oriented person in a culture that tends not to be. I can get frustrated when I try hard to get something started on time, only for key people to be late. My native culture is time-oriented, so I am time-oriented. However, I understand that in my new setting the presence of the full group for an event tends to be a higher cultural value than timeliness.

When people come late to an event, it is almost never considered rude. This even includes major events such as weddings that you would never dream of being late for in the States. Not only is lateness rarely considered rude but, on the contrary, to start before everyone arrives can be considered rude. The public transit system and roadways can be so hectic or unpredictable at times that being late is sometimes just a reality of life. Furthermore, it could be considered rude for someone to cut short their time with another person in order to be on time for their commitment with me.

To not love all aspects of the local culture is okay. If you're being honest, there are some parts of your native culture that you don't like either. The main thing is that you make an effort to understand the local culture and accept it rather than try to impose your native culture on it. Lingenfelter calls this becoming a 150-percent person.[11] He says that before leaving your native culture, you are 100-percent acculturated to that culture. In your new culture, you will probably only become acculturated to about 75 percent of the level of someone who is native to the culture. In the process you will lose some aspects of your native culture, which leaves you 75-percent acculturated there as well. This makes you a 150-percent person, as you are 75-percent acculturated to your native culture and 75-percent acculturated to your new culture. The point here is not the exact percentages; Lingenfelter does not attempt to measure acculturation levels.

---

11   Lingenfelter and Mayers, *Ministering Cross-Culturally*, 24.

His point is that you will not embrace some areas of your new culture, but as long as you make an effort to understand the culture you can still be a great missionary.

10. Maintain some ties to your home culture.
I recently saw an article arguing that missionaries should avoid streaming sports games or TV shows from back home or otherwise maintaining connections to their home culture if they want to adjust to their new culture and overcome culture shock. I don't believe this is entirely true. While it is true that to become assimilated to your new culture you have to give up some of your native culture, as illustrated in Lingenfelter's model of the 150-percent person, I think it is healthy to maintain some ties to home. Using the example of streaming sports games or TV shows, we should recognize that content produced in the United States is widely popular across the globe, and avoiding such content for the sake of becoming more in tune with your new culture when everyone else in that culture is engaging in such content doesn't seem particularly productive. Furthermore, if you cut off all ties to your native culture, it will be more difficult for you to relate to donors and will amplify the reverse culture shock that you experience if you ever move back home, as most missionaries do. You should not spend all of your free time trying to transport yourself back to your home culture through technology, but it is okay to maintain some ties.

11. Maintain a strong relationship with God.
Maintaining a strong relationship with God is the best advice for every season of life, not just when facing a difficult experience such as culture shock. However, it is worth noting that you will do well to find refuge in God during this time. He is the one who called you into this situation, and He will carry you to the other side. Psalm 139:9-10 says, *If I rise on the wings*

*of the dawn, **if I settle on the far side of the sea**, even there your hand will guide me, your right hand will hold me fast* (emphasis added). I discovered this verse as I was preparing to move overseas, and it served as an encouragement to me. I hope it encourages you as well.

The Psalms are riddled with examples of people finding solace in God during difficult times. I encourage you to review the Psalms and find some that can serve as an encouragement to you during this time. Psalm 121 is a perfect example:

> *I lift up my eyes to the mountains –*
> *where does my help come from?*
> *My help comes from the LORD,*
> *the Maker of heaven and earth.*
> *He will not let your foot slip –*
> *he who watches over you will not slumber;*
> *indeed, he who watches over Israel*
> *will neither slumber nor sleep.*
> *The LORD watches over you –*
> *the LORD is your shade at your right hand;*
> *the sun will not harm you by day,*
> *nor the moon by night.*
> *The LORD will keep you from all harm –*
> *he will watch over your life;*
> *the LORD will watch over your coming and going*
> *both now and forevermore.*

Conclusion

In the Bible, it appears quite common for people whom God has chosen for ministry to go through trials before beginning their ministry. Joseph was sold into slavery and then falsely imprisoned. The Israelites traveled through the wilderness before coming to the Promised Land. David ran from Saul. Even Jesus went through forty days in the desert and was tempted by Satan before starting His public ministry.

I call these trials *wilderness experiences* because of the prominence of the literal wilderness in some of the biblical examples, and for many missionaries, culture shock will serve as a wilderness experience. Culture shock is an unfortunate reality that affects everyone who moves overseas. Even though it may seem like a mountain that you will never get over, keep moving forward and don't get discouraged. It will refine you and make your ministry stronger when you come out on the other side. No matter how dark your situation may seem, there is a light at the end of the tunnel. If you put forth a continuous effort to learn your new culture and integrate into it using the recommendations provided here, you will succeed and adapt to your new culture. When you do, you will have an incredible experience and an awesome ministry waiting for you. Trust me, it is worth enduring to see what awaits on the other side.

Chapter 7

Beyond Culture Shock – Doing Culturally Informed Ministry

Surviving culture shock is an important hurdle in mission work, but whereas culture shock is a short-lived phase of your time abroad, if you continue as a missionary for the long term, the need to have a culturally informed ministry never goes away. The gospel message and the Bible are universally true and universally applicable. However, the nuances of how ministry is done from one culture to another can differ without diluting the core message. This is known as *contextualization*, defined by missiologists Tom Steffan and Lois Douglas as "taking the gospel to a new context and finding appropriate ways to communicate it so that it is understandable to the people in that context."[12]

Missiologists David Hesselgrave and Edward Rommen offer a slightly different definition that is also beneficial for understanding the term. "Contextualization entails entering a cultural context, discerning what God is doing and saying in

---

12   Tom A. Steffen and Lois McKinney Douglas, *Encountering Missionary Life and Work: Preparing for Intercultural Ministry* (Grand Rapids, MI: Baker Academic, 2008), 39.

that context, and speaking and working for needed change."[13] In other words, contextualization is about showing the relevance of the gospel within a particular context. You have probably heard churches talk about the importance of making the gospel relevant, and while I appreciate this sentiment, I think it is more accurate to use the phrase "showing the relevance of the gospel" rather than "making the gospel relevant." The gospel is already relevant and does not need us to add to or take away from it to make it relevant. What we need to do, though, is show the relevance of the gospel, which is not obvious to everyone at first glance.

I once had a missionary to Mexico tell me that he thought missionaries had done more harm than good in Mexico. This was not an atheist or someone who was antagonistic towards the gospel; he was a Christian missionary who believed enough in missions to dedicate his life to it. His reason for saying this is that he felt Western missionaries had imposed Western culture on Mexico more than they had advanced God's kingdom. While I am inclined to believe that this individual was exaggerating, it is possible to have your understanding of Christianity so woven with your culture that you unintentionally advance your culture rather than the gospel while serving abroad.

An extreme example of this can be seen during the colonial period, when European conquistadors forced indigenous peoples to "convert" to Christianity. However, more subtle forms of cultural disregard and ethnocentrism can creep into missions if we are not careful. For example, a missionary to North Africa once shared a story of a group that decided to build a bathroom for a community that had no bathrooms. The missionaries had great intentions, but after spending time and money to build the bathroom facilities, no one from the village

---

13   David J. Hesselgrave and Edward W. Rommen, *Contextualization: Meanings, Methods, and Models* (Pasadena, CA: William Carey Library, 2000), 150.

used them. They all continued to wander off to a secluded spot to do their business as they had before. It turned out that the villagers thought the idea of everyone going to the bathroom in the same place was disgusting.

These missionaries didn't cause any real harm to the community they were working in, but they didn't cause much help either. In the end, they wasted time, energy, and resources on a project that seemed important from the perspective of their native culture but was viewed differently by the local culture. Furthermore, it is possible that they damaged relationships with the local community by implying that their culture was superior to the local culture. Think about it. How would you feel if someone showed up in your community and started a building project that no one in the community wanted and then tried to get everyone to use what they had built? You would probably find the person a nuisance, or at the very least, you would be apathetic toward their work. You certainly wouldn't be endeared toward them or interested in hearing a message that they wanted to share with you.

Whenever you enter a new culture, you should always adopt the posture of a learner rather than a teacher. If the missionaries in this example had taken the time to learn what the community saw as an important project rather than launching into their own presuppositions of what was needed, this story would have turned out differently. We see this principle of starting with a learner mentality in both of the aforementioned definitions for contextualization, with the first emphasizing the need to find (learn) appropriate ways to communicate the gospel message, and the second encouraging one to discern (learn) what God is doing in that context. Regardless of how long you are in ministry, you can always learn more. None of us have infinite knowledge, so openness to learn about the culture and ministry is always a good practice.

This does not mean that it is never appropriate to disagree with or challenge cultural presuppositions. Once you have learned and become ingrained in the local culture, you have earned the right to critique it as you would critique your own culture. The core teachings of Jesus tend to be countercultural regardless of what culture you are in. For example, I can't think of any culture where it is natural to love one's enemies. Christian ministry will always involve challenging the norm to a certain extent, which is the final step of contextualization according to Hesselgrave and Rommen; it is "speaking and working for needed change."

As you learn about your new culture, you will find that different cultures interpret biblical passages differently. As much as we may try to objectively understand the Bible, all of us are subject to what one of my professors used to call a flawed filter. When we read a passage of Scripture, we naturally filter our understanding through our life experiences and cultural background without even realizing it. That filter is flawed, though, because humanity is sinful. The result is that cultural presuppositions can influence biblical interpretation, theology, and church structure.

One example of this is church governance. In the Christian circles that I have been a part of in the United States, churches often have bylaws which require the congregation to vote on major decisions, including, but not limited to, hiring a new pastor. In the church of the New Testament, though, we never see an occasion of the congregation voting on a decision. Rather, major decisions were always made by appointed leaders such as apostles, elders, and deacons. This does not mean that the model of congregational voting is sinful, but it must be acknowledged that this model is more reflective of American democratic ideals than biblical examples of church governance.

Another example that has struck me during my time as

a missionary is how the command to honor one's father and mother is understood across cultures. In the United States, I had always understood this to mean that one must respect his or her parents. However, in El Salvador, where the culture is much more communal and one's independent actions can bring honor or shame to the family unit, the command to honor one's father and mother is understood to include not engaging in bad behavior that will bring dishonor to one's parents. A person who doesn't mistreat his or her parents but lives unhinged could therefore be understood in the United States as fulfilling the command to honor one's mother and father, but not in El Salvador.

To be clear, I do not believe that truth is relative or culturally dependent. I believe in absolute truth, but our understanding of that truth is imperfect since we are imperfect. This means that we must approach the Bible with humility and ask the Holy Spirit to reveal to us the truth of the Word that He inspired. You do not have to accept every theological norm of the Christian churches in your new culture, because part of speaking and working for needed change means addressing inaccurate theology. However, be sure to take the time to understand the perspective of your new culture before you try to correct it. When you find differences in theology between your home culture and your new culture, you should consider the possibility that your new culture is the one that has the better understanding. If you side with your home culture every time you recognize a difference, you may be guilty of ethnocentrism.

I experienced an incident that illustrates the importance of understanding a culture's perspective rather than condemning it at first glance. When I arrived at the prison ministry in El Salvador, it bothered me whenever I heard a pastor or Christian leader insinuate that Christians should dress formally. I couldn't understand why such an emphasis was put on outward appearance when we serve a God who looks at the heart. It didn't make sense until one of the pastors explained the reasoning behind this. The pastor agreed that dressing formally is not biblically mandated for Christians, and he did not think it was sinful to dress informally. However, since all of the Christians in the prison had former gang affiliations, he encouraged the Christians to dress formally because people would look to see if they still had ties to the gang when they returned to their communities. If they continued to don the baggy, unkempt clothing style of the gang, they would be perceived as being in the gang, and this could put their lives in jeopardy. Therefore, he encouraged the Christians to dress formally to create the greatest distinction possible to indicate that they were no longer in the gang. His position was not one of legalism but practical, culturally informed advice to keep people safe. Had I attacked this position without understanding it, I would have unwittingly come down on someone who was simply trying to help people.

Cross-Cultural Ministry in the Bible

The Bible gives us many examples of cross-cultural ministry that we can learn from. In the Old Testament, we see people like Joseph, Daniel, Nehemiah, and Esther serving in God-ordained ministries in foreign cultures. In the New Testament, we see Jesus ministering to Samaritans, Philip evangelizing the Ethiopian eunuch, and Peter preaching the gospel to Cornelius. Perhaps the biblical figure that we most think of when we consider cross-cultural missionaries is Paul. Paul was a Jew who was so deeply entrenched in the Jewish way of life that he killed those whom he thought posed a threat to Jewish beliefs. Describing his high degree of Jewishness later in life, Paul said in Philippians, *If someone else thinks they have reasons to put* *confidence in the flesh, I have more: circumcised on the eighth day, of the people of Israel, of the tribe of Benjamin, **a Hebrew of Hebrews**; in regard to the law, a Pharisee; as for zeal, persecuting the church; as for righteousness based on the law, faultless* (Philippians 3:4-6, emphasis added).

Despite being *a Hebrew of Hebrews*, Paul's primary ministry was to the Gentiles, a broad-reaching term that included anyone who was not Jewish. The second half of Acts is dedicated almost entirely to his missionary journeys throughout the Roman world. Every church he planted was located outside the territory of Israel, and every letter he wrote that we have on record was directed to people outside the territory of Israel. Several key passages in Paul's ministry give us a helpful model of cross-cultural ministry.

The first instance we notice is the Jerusalem Council in Acts 15. This comes at the end of Paul and Barnabas's first missionary journey, when newcomers at their sending church of Antioch taught that one must be circumcised to be a follower of Jesus. Circumcision is the only law mentioned in the initial argument, but the remainder of the chapter indicates that although this was the main point of dispute, these individuals were likely teaching that the Law of Moses must be observed in order for one to be a Christian. The disagreement between these two parties was so great that it prompted a meeting between the apostles and Christian leaders to determine what would become the official position of the church.

It is important to highlight the cultural underpinnings of this dispute. The Law of Moses was not just part of religious practice, but also served as a centerpiece of Jewish society. Being a good Jew and observing the Law of Moses were inextricably connected. For this reason, when Paul describes his history in the Jewish culture in Philippians 3, his evidence of his Jewishness is the care with which he observed the Law of

Moses. Therefore, those who were causing turmoil in Antioch were not merely waging a theological disagreement but were also insinuating that for a Gentile to be a follower of Jesus, he or she must abandon his or her native culture and adopt Jewish culture.

Ultimately, the Jerusalem Council concluded that there was no need for Gentiles to observe the ritual elements of the Law of Moses. In order words, it was not necessary for Gentiles to abandon their culture and adopt Jewish culture in order to become Christians. In the same way, modern missionaries will do well to avoid trying to get converts to adopt Western culture when they become Christians. This is rarely done intentionally; usually missionaries have good motivations. Even in the example of Acts 15, the motivation of the believers whom Paul and Barnabas contradicted is not clearly stated; they may simply have wanted to help the believers at Antioch grow closer to God based on their own understanding of what that meant.

However, regardless of what the motivation was, the result was deemed to be damaging. It is described by Peter as *putting on the necks of Gentiles a yoke that neither we nor our ancestors have been able to bear* (Acts 15:10). Similarly, modern-day missionaries must be careful not to infuse their native culture into their ministry to such an extent that they end up creating converts to Western culture as much as they create converts to Christianity.

It is also interesting to examine the four commands from the Law of Moses that the Jerusalem Council concluded should be preserved by the Gentiles. The command to abstain from sexual immorality is obviously a moral one that is repeated throughout Scripture. The other three commands appear to be ritual commands regarding eating practices. One of these, the command to abstain from food sacrificed to idols, is specifically addressed by Paul in 1 Corinthians 8, and we learn from

Paul's comments that eating such food was not sinful in and of itself. Paul says quite explicitly, *But food does not bring us near to God; we are no worse if we do not eat, and no better if we do* (1 Corinthians 8:8). If eating meat sacrificed to idols was morally permissible, why, then, was it restricted in the conclusion of the Jerusalem Council?

Based on the rest of Paul's comments in his epistle to the church of Corinth, the most logical explanation for not eating food sacrificed to idols is that this restriction was intended to foster unity. Meals appear to have been a large part of Christian fellowship in the early church, as indicated by Acts 2:46, which states that the believers *broke bread in their homes and ate together* daily. If certain eating practices were known to cause contention, the council deemed it best to avoid these to prevent causing a brother to stumble in the faith. As in the example of clothing styles that I shared from my personal experience, the command was intended as a practical way to serve a higher purpose rather than a universal determination of right and wrong.

Applying this principle, we can say that modern-day missionaries should strive to maintain unity and avoid unnecessary dissension by adhering to cultural norms as much as possible, with the exception of any norm that is sinful, in order to serve the higher purpose of making disciples. For example, in some cultures dogs are looked down upon. You might be a dog lover like me, but if you want to host people in your home in such a culture, having a dog as a pet may prove to be a hindrance. Or, if you are a missionary in a culture where cows are considered sacred, you will probably burn some bridges with the people you want to reach if you eat beef in public. Eating beef is perfectly permissible biblically, but not doing so is also permissible. However, if eating beef publicly will create an unnecessary barrier to people accepting your message, refraining from doing so will show respect for the local beliefs and make people more open to hearing the gospel message.

This does not mean that you should succumb to norms that are going to hinder your ministry. It is also important to make a distinction between norms in a specific Christian tradition and broader cultural norms. For example, in the more conservative churches of El Salvador, it is not uncommon to consider playing sports sinful. While this is a norm in a specific Christian tradition, it is not a norm across Christianity in general, nor is it a norm within Salvadoran culture in general. Therefore, we continue to operate a large soccer ministry. If we were to succumb to the norm that is present in some churches of not playing sports, this would hinder our ministry, since it would prevent us from continuing one of the main vehicles we currently use to convey the gospel.

Deciding what norms should be accepted and what should be rejected can be answered by two simple questions. First, is it morally sinful for me to do this? Second, will doing this hurt or help serve the goal of making disciples? If the practice in question is not morally sinful but aids the goal of making disciples, we should adopt this practice. If it is either morally sinful or hurts the goal of making disciples, we should reject it.

This brings us to the second key passage from Paul's life in which he shares his personal philosophy of cross-cultural ministry. Paul builds upon his discussion of whether to eat food sacrificed to idols:

> *Though I am free and belong to no one, I have made myself a slave to everyone, to win as many as possible. To the Jews I became like a Jew, to win the Jews. To those under the law I became like one under the law (though I myself am not under the law), so as to win those under the law. To those not having the law*

I became like one not having the law (though I am not free from God's law but am under Christ's law), so as to win those not having the law. To the weak I became weak, to win the weak. I have become all things to all people so that by all possible means I might save some. I do all this for the sake of the gospel, that I may share in its blessings. (1 Corinthians 9:19-23)

Paul is saying that in whatever context he entered, he adopted the norms of that context because it enabled him to reach more people with the gospel message. When he was with Gentiles, he adopted their cultural norms in order to contextualize the gospel for them. When he was with Jews, he reverted to Jewish cultural norms in order to contextualize the gospel for them. With his caveat – *though I myself am not under the law* – Paul makes it clear that he was not doing this because of moral necessity but rather as a ministry strategy *so that by all possible means I might save some.*

We see an excellent example of Paul putting this into practice in Acts 17:16-34. In this passage, Paul is in the city of Athens awaiting Silas and Timothy's arrival, who had stayed behind in Berea to finish a work they had begun there. Rather than sit idly waiting for them to arrive so they could continue their missionary journey together, Paul decides to use this as an opportunity to evangelize the city. As the text progresses, Paul engages in all of the steps of contextualization that were presented in the definitions at the beginning of this chapter. First, he begins going to the market every day to spark conversations with the people he meets. All this time that he evangelizes, he learns about the local culture. When a group of philosophers learn of Paul's preaching, their interest is piqued, and they invite him to speak at their next gathering at the Areopagus.

As Paul begins his sermon, we see the depth of his cultural

discovery journey: *I walked around and looked carefully at your objects of worship* (Acts 17:23). Paul spent time specifically dedicated to understanding the culture of Athens. He did this with intentionality, as evidenced by the word *carefully*. At some point he must have studied philosophy as well, because in Acts 17:28 he quotes two separate philosophers who would have been known and respected by this audience.

By showing his cultural understanding, Paul earns the right to speak and work for needed change. He makes this jump into the final part of contextualization when he notes that in the city there was a statue dedicated to an unknown God; he then proceeds to share with them that Jesus is precisely this unknown God. The goal of a missionary is not merely to understand a culture or give discourses that show this understanding. The goal of a missionary is to present the gospel in a way that can be easily understood in the cultural context. Without arriving at this final step, any cultural acquisition is meaningless from a mission perspective.

Conclusion

Cross-cultural ministry is a necessary component of fulfilling the Great Commission, but it presents unique challenges that one does not face in monocultural ministries. Coming into a new culture always requires missionaries to take the time to learn and study their new cultural context in order to discern how they can present the gospel in a way that will be most easily understood and accepted within the host culture. This is known as contextualization and can be seen in cross-cultural ministry in the Bible as well as in effective modern-day ministries. Missionaries who ignore the importance of culture will find their ministries less fruitful even though they may have a great understanding of the Bible and great intentions. For this reason, as missionaries we must consciously consider how we can incarnate the message of the gospel in the best way possible in our new cultures.

Chapter 8

Personal Spiritual Health

Many people view missionaries as super-Christians who are on fire for God and could never possibly go through a spiritual dry spell. This is far from reality. Missionaries are people like any other Christians, and they share the same tendency to grow cold if they are not stoking the flame of faith in their lives. It can be easy to neglect your personal spiritual care when you are active in vocational ministry. For example, you might justify not having a personal devotional time reading the Bible when you know you're constantly preparing Bible studies, or you might justify cutting time in personal prayer when you know you'll be praying with people throughout the week. Likewise, you could justify not going to church on Sunday when you've spent the rest of the week in ministry. The list of examples goes on and on. In this chapter, allow me to share some biblical principles and practical advice for maintaining a strong personal spiritual life as a missionary.

Almost ten years ago, I was introduced to a concept that forever shifted my perception of ministry. God does not want you to do ministry *for* Him but rather *with* Him. We often talk about doing things for God or going into ministry to serve God; there is nothing wrong with this in and of itself. However, doing things *for* God without also doing them *with* God is futile. One of the clearest biblical examples of this can be seen in Luke 10:38-42 when Jesus visits the home of Martha and Mary. Martha works diligently to ensure that He has the best visit possible. The text describes this in verse 40, saying that she *was distracted by all the preparations that had to be made.* Mary, on the other hand, was doing nothing to assist with the household chores. She simply sat at the feet of Jesus listening to what He said.

If you've ever had roommates, you know how frustrated people can get when they feel like they do all of the work to care for the house or apartment while everyone else sits back and rests. My most explosive arguments with roommates have always been over the distribution of cleaning responsibilities. Martha apparently felt this way, and after reaching a boiling point, she decided it was time to employ Jesus to convince Mary to do her share of the work. Jesus' response must have caught Martha off guard. We read in verses 41-42:

> *"Martha, Martha,"* the Lord answered, *"you are worried and upset about many things, but few things are needed—or indeed only one. Mary has chosen what is better, and it will not be taken away from her."*

Every time I read this story, I relate to Martha. I love having a checklist of tasks that I can complete one after the other. By accomplishing enough tasks, I feel like I have made good use of my time. This, however, is not the mindset that Jesus praises in this passage. There's nothing wrong with the tasks themselves that Martha is doing. After all, she is making preparations for Jesus so He can have the best visit possible, but while Martha is busy doing things *for* Jesus, Mary is spending her time *with* Jesus. Jesus' response indicates that being *with* Him is far greater than anything done *for* Him.

We can conclude that your personal relationship with God is far more important than anything you could do for Him in ministry. Therefore, it is better for you to take care of your own spiritual health at the expense of some ministry tasks than for you to run a million miles an hour to facilitate a seemingly thriving ministry while your own relationship with God suffers.

We see another example of this concept in Exodus 33. In the preceding chapters, Moses has received God's laws and precepts for the Israelites on Mount Sinai. Suddenly, this meeting between Moses and God is interrupted as God commands Moses to return to the people because they have made a golden calf as an idol that they are worshiping. When he descends the mountain and sees the Israelites' idol worship, Moses is so infuriated that he shatters the tablets on which God had inscribed the commandments. Arriving at chapter 33, we see the conversation between God and Moses in the immediate aftermath of this event. Notice verse 3 in which God says to Moses, *"Go up to the land flowing with milk and honey. But I will not go with you, because you are a stiff-necked people and I might destroy you on the way."*

God was going to allow the people to proceed to the Promised Land, but He would not go with them. Moses would continue to serve God in the leadership position that God had ordained for him, but he would be merely working *for* God rather than walking in step *with* God. Moses' response in verses 15-16 is unwavering:

> *"If your Presence does not go with us, do not send us up from here. How will anyone know that you are pleased with me and with your people unless you*

*go with us? What else will distinguish me and your
people from all the other people on the face of the
earth?"*

The Promised Land is described in the book of Exodus as a
paradise, a land flowing with milk and honey. It was a land of
great prosperity and abundance. God was promising Moses
and the Israelites safe passage to, and conquest of, this land.
Many people would jump at the chance to have a blessing of
this magnitude, but Moses recognized that the blessing would
be meaningless if not accompanied by the presence of the
Blesser. He said without hesitation that it would be better for
them to forgo this blessing of the Promised Land and remain
in the harsh, arid conditions of the desert wilderness if it meant
having the presence of God with them. God's response in verse
17 indicates that He is pleased with Moses' request: *"I will do
the very thing you have asked, because I am pleased with you
and I know you by name."* He then continues to lead and guide
the Israelites rather than abandon them as He had proposed.

Moses held a deep conviction that any blessing one could
receive from God, no matter how grandiose and incredible, is
meaningless in comparison to the blessing of God's presence
itself. Is your desire for God's presence this strong? If God
blessed your ministry with incredible fruitfulness, but you
had no communion with Him, would you be satisfied? These
questions are as challenging to me as I hope they are for you.
We must do everything we can to foster a strong personal relationship with God and recognize that everything else in our
lives, including our ministries, is secondary.

Spiritual Disciplines for Missionaries

Even though this section is entitled "Spiritual Disciplines for Missionaries," the disciplines discussed here apply to any Christian. A spiritual discipline is defined as a habit that one practices for the purpose of growing closer to God. Just as exercise habits foster physical strength and study habits increase our mental capacities, spiritual habits or disciplines increase our spiritual strength. These five habits will keep you spiritually healthy:

- Daily Bible time

- Prayer

- Rest

- Fasting

- Church involvement

The first habit that every missionary must have to continue in growth is a daily time of Bible reading. I prefer to do this in the morning, before my mind is distracted by the stresses of the day. I find that this helps to frame my mind for the remainder of the day. As part of this discipline, I recommend a Bible-reading plan that directs your reading each day. For years I did not do this, but chose books of the Bible at random to read during my devotional time. I didn't realize the problem with this until one of my pastors pointed it out to me. I had read certain books repeatedly and I knew them well, but I had never read other portions of the Bible even once. Everyone has favorite books of the Bible, so if you choose what you read randomly without having a set plan, you tend to read these books over and over while neglecting those you find more difficult. This could result in an unbalanced theology in which your understanding of the

Bible is based only on certain passages that you enjoy, rather than the Bible as a whole. If you need a Bible-reading plan, you can find one through an online search, on the website YouVersion[14] or by asking your pastor. You can even create your own. One of the most popular ones I am aware of is the Life Journal, which comes with a journal that is intended to be used for reflecting on the reading each day. Whether you use this plan or not, you may find that it helps to journal about the passages you read or highlight verses that stand out to you. Your exact method of Bible reading is up to you, but daily time in the Scriptures is essential.

In addition to reading the Bible, your daily devotional time should include a time of focused prayer. It is good to pray throughout the day, as you go about your ministry or anything else you may do. However, an additional time that you carve out specifically for God to realign you with His desires for your life is also necessary. This is the main purpose of prayer. While it is great to bring requests before God, and the Bible has many examples of people doing this, the main purpose of prayer is to bring yourself into alignment with God's heart. An example of this is Jesus' teaching on prayer in Matthew 6:9-13, which has come to be known as the Lord's Prayer:

> *"This, then, is how you should pray:*
> *'Our Father in heaven,*
> *hallowed be your name,*
> *your kingdom come,*
> *your will be done,*
> *on earth as it is in heaven.*
> *Give us today our daily bread.*
> *And forgive us our debts,*

---

14   "The Bible App," *YouVersion, https://www.youversion.com/the-bible-app/* (October 30, 2020).

as we also have forgiven our debtors.
And lead us not into temptation,
but deliver us from the evil one.'"

The bulk of this prayer is dedicated to bringing the praying person into greater alignment with God's purposes. First, the prayer recognizes who God is. Second, there is the request for His kingdom to come and His will to be done, both of which serve as examples of the person seeking God's purpose in their personal life and in the world at large. The next sentence is a request for a specific need, but then the prayer turns back to personal alignment with God as the person asks for forgiveness. The acts of confession and repentance are recognitions that they have become misaligned with God and want to be realigned. We also see that Jesus reminds them to forgive others, thus reflecting on God's precepts. Finally, the last sentence begins with the person asking God to lead them and more specifically to guard them against temptation. In other words, the person is asking God to help them avoid becoming misaligned with Him again. Then, the prayer ends with the person asking God to deliver them from the Evil One. As you can see, the primary purpose of this prayer is alignment with God.

The third spiritual discipline that missionaries should engage in is rest. It may be odd to think of rest as a spiritual discipline, but there is biblical precedence to consider it as such. When many people think of missionaries, they picture saints who dedicate all of their time to ministry. The reality, though, is that missionaries, like vocational ministers back home, are not engaged in their ministry role 24/7. You will have free time like anyone else, and if you don't, you will burn out quickly and not last long in ministry. Taking time to rest is a biblical principle first illustrated by God when He rested on the seventh day of creation, and later when He included the Sabbath as a day of rest in the Ten Commandments. When you think about this, it's actually quite incredible. The Ten Commandments have the reputation of containing some of the most important instructions in the entire Torah. Included in them are commands against sins like murder, adultery, and worshiping idols that we would consider a big deal. Right in the midst of this list, though, is a command to honor the Sabbath as a holy day of rest. The command was so serious that failure to observe the Sabbath could be punished by exile or even death (Exodus 31:14). Not only do we often overlook this, but we even look down on resting at times.

Even Jesus took time out of His public ministry to rest. In Luke 5:15-16, a passage that shows both the importance of an active prayer life and the importance of rest, we read, *Yet the news about him spread all the more, so that crowds of people came to hear him and to be healed of their sicknesses. But Jesus often withdrew to lonely places and prayed.* Jesus' ministry grew rapidly. He drew huge crowds and garnered a large following. Many of us would think we need to push ourselves harder, block out other activities in our lives, and capitalize on the momentum of such progress. It is at precisely this point, though, that Luke highlights Jesus' intentionality in withdrawing for times of rest and seeking God. If Jesus needed this practice, we certainly do as well.

Fasting is the fourth spiritual discipline that missionaries should practice. Fasting is a bit of a lost art, and it is common in modern society for people to "fast" from something that is not as difficult as food. Fasting is presented as an important practice in both the Old and New Testaments, and the model for fasting that is routinely presented in the Bible is giving up food. This is not to say, for example, that spending less time on social media and more time praying is by any means bad.

However, while this may be a good practice, I am not sure that this constitutes a fast. Fasting is a form of humbling ourselves before God in order to seek a deeper relationship with Him and/or to present a specific need to Him. Not eating serves this purpose of humbling ourselves because it reminds us of our own fragility in a way that giving up non-essential items does not.

If you are nearing your departure for the mission field, I would recommend that you consider fasting once a week to pray for this transition. Perhaps you may want to employ a few close friends to fast with you as well. Even after you arrive at your ministry assignment, don't give up fasting. You might not continue doing it every week, and you might want to take some time without fasting as your body adjusts to new food, new bacteria, and a new climate. However, fasting should be a discipline that you practice throughout your ministry and beyond.

The fifth spiritual discipline that you should practice is local church involvement. This is one of the easiest disciplines to neglect as a missionary; when you've been active in ministry all week, congregating on Sundays might not seem as important. You might try to justify that you fellowship with Christians throughout the week during the ministry and go to Bible studies as part of the ministry. This is the purpose of going to church, so a missionary might not feel the need to become part of a local church as well.

I disagree with this reasoning and argue that regardless of your ministerial role, it is still important to be part of a local church, which includes regular attendance at the church's main service, whether that takes place on a Sunday or a Saturday. I would also add that watching services online from your church back home does not replace the need to be involved in a local church. Watching church services from back home is great, and I am thankful that technology allows modern missionaries to do this. However, it is still important to be involved in a church in your local context.

During Jesus' lifetime and throughout the book of Acts, the biblical concept of the Sabbath was understood to include congregating in the synagogue, and both Jesus and Paul appear to have been regular attendees at these gatherings. This is the model from which the modern practice of weekly church services originates, and it makes sense that if Jesus practiced this, we should too. Furthermore, Hebrews 10:24-25 commands us in this regard:

> *And let us consider how we may spur one another on toward love and good deeds, **not giving up meeting together, as some are in the habit of doing** – and all the more as you see the Day approaching.*
> (emphasis added)

While this command is not limited to Sunday church services and makes no mention of a particular day, it does make it clear that all Christians should be part of a church community with whom they regularly gather. It is hard to see how you can be part of a church community without participating in their most predominant gatherings, which in modern society tends to be the Sunday service.

Even if you disagree with me that it is necessary to be part of a local church in addition to your mission work, I still recommend that you join one to set an example for the people you are discipling. Although you may be surrounded by Christians and engaged in ministry every day as you do mission work, the majority of Christians work more traditional jobs and only have the local church to serve as their form of Christian community. If the people you are trying to reach and disciple see that you're not attending a church, in all likelihood they won't either.

The Bible teaches on multiple occasions that leaders will be held to a higher standard. James 3:1 is one of the most famous examples of this, stating clearly: *Not many of you should become teachers, my fellow believers, because you know that we who teach will be judged more strictly.* Even if you don't think of yourself as a teacher, almost everyone in vocational ministry is involved in some level of teaching, and you most certainly qualify as a leader. You should be encouraging the people you disciple to be part of a local church, and as a leader that means that you should be part of a local church too.

One other reason that missionaries should be part of a local church is so that there is a context in which they can receive rather than just give. In the course of mission work, you are constantly pouring yourself out in your time and energy. Being part of a local church is your chance to refill your spiritual tank. You can receive biblical teaching, engage in communal worship, have people pray for you, and spend time with other Christians in a context where you can relax and not feel like you are always the one imparting truth. If you continually pour yourself out without refilling, you will burn out quickly and may not be in ministry very long. If you have a rigorous ministry schedule already, being part of a local church does not necessarily mean that you have to take on added responsibilities within the church. If you decide that you want to, that's certainly great, but make sure you retain some context within the church where you can simply receive and recharge.

In addition to attending Sunday services, you should consider joining a small group in your church. Sunday services are for communal worship and receiving biblical preaching, but they do not do as much to foster relationships between church members as small groups do. If you want to get to know people in the church and not just be an attender on Sundays, a small group is the best way to accomplish that. Also, a small group connection early in your time abroad can help mitigate culture shock by providing you with local friendships, which I have already noted is important.

Some mission organizations require their missionaries to attend a particular church, but missionaries often have the liberty to choose their own church. If you find yourself in this situation, you need to know what criteria to consider. Should you limit your search to the communities where you work or the churches that partner with your ministry? Should you look for a church that feels like home? Should you look for a church that holds services in your native language or in your local language? All of these are valid questions that I have considered during my time as a missionary. I concluded that you should go to whatever church you feel the most comfortable in; you need to be enthusiastic about joining that group. In other words, you should choose a church that you believe will help you to recharge and grow spiritually regardless of whether it is located in the communities where you minister or affiliated with your organization in some way.

I recommend that you ask the others in your ministry if you can visit their churches with them when you first arrive, as this can be a great way to find a church if you are new to the area. However, don't feel obligated to choose one of these churches as your home church if you discover another that you think is a better fit for you. If you live in a metropolitan area, most likely at least one church will have services in English, and you may want to consider being part of such a church until you are comfortable in your understanding of the local language. However, you must not assume that just because a church uses your native language, it will feel like your church back home. There is much more to a church than the language that is spoken, and in my experience, the churches that have felt most like home have ironically not been English-speaking churches.

A final issue for missionaries to consider regarding churches is where they should give their tithe. Should you tithe to your church back home, to the church you attend locally, or divide the tithe between them? Some mission organizations have policies regarding this or require you to tithe a certain percentage to the denomination. If the decision is up to you, though, I would encourage you to continue tithing to your church back home until you find a local church; then tithe to that local church. Without making a biblical defense of tithing, as that is not the purpose of this book, I believe that your tithe should generally go to whatever church you have joined locally. If you happen to be in a developing country, as many missionaries are, your tithe will probably do more to help in your local context than it will back home.

Although not necessarily a spiritual discipline, I believe that a final practice that is worth noting here is the importance of avoiding temptation. It is easiest to give in to temptation when we are stressed, overwhelmed, disappointed, or anxious. This array of emotions is common for new missionaries, and the fact that you are away from home can compound the ease with which you give in to temptation because you feel like no one will ever know. Sin always seems small at its onset, but it inevitably grows if it is not addressed – and will eventually destroy your ministry, your personal life, your relationships, your family, and everything that you hold dear. The longer you give in to temptation, the harder it becomes to kill the sin. It may feel like a stress release for a moment, but it will eventually hunt you down and take you out if you keep flirting with it. In Genesis 4:7, God said to Cain, *"Sin is crouching at your door; it desires to have you, but you must rule over it."* Cain never gained mastery over his sin, and in the end, it destroyed him. The same applies to both you and me.

Burnout: How to Prevent It and How to Overcome It

A final topic that should be discussed concerning personal spiritual health is how to prevent burnout and how to overcome it if you're already there. Burnout is defined as "fatigue, frustration, or apathy resulting from prolonged stress, overwork, or intense activity."[15] I would hypothesize that most people experience burnout at some point in their lives, and even if you have never experienced this, you can probably think of someone whom you have suspected of being burned out. Preventing yourself from getting to this place and overcoming this phenomenon as soon as possible if you are there is important, because you cannot minister as effectively or fulfill with excellence your other roles in life such as being a spouse, parent, or friend if you are burned out. Staying faithful to the aforementioned spiritual disciplines will help to prevent burnout, but it is worth looking at some additional passages that address this.

Two of the foremost prophets in the Old Testament are Moses and Elijah. Their importance in Scripture is evidenced by the fact that they are the only two prophets to appear with Jesus at the transfiguration (Matthew 17:3; Mark 9:4; Luke 9:30). Both had incredible ministries that still impact us today, yet both were subject to the same pressures of ministry that we experience.

In Exodus 18 we read of a visit that Moses received from his father-in-law, Jethro, while leading the Israelites through the wilderness. Upon his arrival, Jethro discovered that Moses was spending his entire day judging disputes among the people. Jethro confronted Moses regarding this in verses 17-18:

---

15   "Burnout." *Dictionary.com. https://www.dictionary.com/browse/burnout?s=t* (April 22, 2020).

"What you are doing is not good. You and these people who come to you will only wear yourselves out. The work is too heavy for you; you cannot handle it alone."

Jethro gave his reason for this in verse 19. *"You must be the people's representative before God and bring their disputes to him."*

In other words, Jethro recognized that God had called Moses to lead the people and represent them before Him, not to settle menial disputes. Moses needed to allow others to do this work so that he could focus on what God had called him to do. If not, he was going to burn out.

This passage reveals an important ministry principle. No one can do it all, and no one is called to do it all. God has called and gifted you with a specific role in His kingdom. He has called others to different roles. As Paul says in 1 Corinthians 12:12, *Just as a body, though one, has many parts, but all its many parts form one body, so it is with Christ.* He then goes on to ask in verses 29-30, *Are all apostles? Are all prophets? Are all teachers? Do all work miracles? Do all have gifts of healing? Do all speak in tongues? Do all interpret?* The implied answer, of course, is no. Everyone has their own role to fill. Focus on the calling God has given you. When you assume responsibilities that go beyond the role God has called you to fill and try to navigate them in addition to your God-ordained ministry responsibilities, you will have a higher likelihood of burning out.

As your ministry grows, you must learn how to delegate responsibilities to others. Not every responsibility can be delegated. In Moses' case, being *the people's representative before God* could not be delegated. Settling disputes could, and Moses ultimately does this at Jethro's advice. If you are working to the point that you feel burned out, you may be holding on to some tasks that could be delegated to others.

We see a similar story in Acts 6. At this point in the story of the early church, the number of believers was greatly increasing. The church had developed a food distribution ministry for widows, but with the amount of growth that was taking place, complaints arose that some of the widows were being overlooked. After gathering to discuss this, the twelve apostles arrived at their conclusion in verses 2-4:

> *"It would not be right for us to neglect the ministry of the word of God in order to wait on tables. Brothers and sisters, choose seven men from among you who are known to be full of the Spirit and wisdom. We will turn this responsibility over to them and will give our attention to prayer and the ministry of the word."*

The ministry of aiding widows was extremely important in the early church. There is no shortage of verses in the Bible commanding the people of God to care for widows. However, despite its importance, the twelve apostles recognized that this particular ministry was not the assignment that God had given them. As a result, they chose to delegate this responsibility to others even though it was important. Because they did this instead of trying to balance all of the needs of the church by themselves, a new office of the church was born, and others were empowered to do ministry as well.

If you are a missionary, you will constantly be presented with needs and ministry opportunities. If you say yes to every one of them, you will soon find yourself in the same position as Moses and the apostles. There was a time in my life when I was a yes man; I would say yes to most requests and hated saying no to anyone. I have since learned that this is neither realistic nor healthy. You need to be laser-locked focused on

God's calling for your life, pursue it with everything you are, and feel the liberty to say no to anything that goes beyond or falls outside of that purpose. When your load becomes too heavy, determine what you can delegate to others. If you don't do this, you will soon have more responsibilities than you can handle and burn out before you fulfill what God has called you to do.

You may object and fear that if you decline to address a need, no one else will meet it. While it is easy to think this way, it is rarely true. If there is a legitimate need that God wants to meet, He is capable of raising up any number of people to fill it. You are not so important as to be the determining factor. Also, if you try to fill a ministry role that you are not called to fill, you may be standing in the way of the person that God wants to use in that ministry.

Let's turn now to Elijah, who had the most severe encounter with burnout recorded in Scripture. As we have already noted, Elijah is a hugely important figure in the Bible. By the time of Jesus, he may even have been considered the most important prophet in Hebrew history other than Moses. John the Baptist was repeatedly likened to Elijah (Matthew 11:14; 17:12; Luke 1:17). Jesus preached about Elijah (Luke 4:25-26). Some of those among Jesus' crowds of followers believed Him to be a second coming of Elijah (Matthew 16:14). Elijah appeared with Jesus at the transfiguration (Matthew 17:3; Mark 9:4; Luke 9:30), and when Jesus called out in prayer as He was being crucified, some onlookers assumed He was calling Elijah (Matthew 27:47). However, in 1 Kings 19 we find Elijah in full-fledged burnout, hiding alone in a cave and complaining to God that his life is so miserable it would be better for him to die.

The timing of this crisis in Elijah's life is quite astonishing. Elijah had just defeated the prophets of Baal in dramatic fashion at Mount Carmel, which included an unequivocal miracle that God performed on his behalf. Some consider this to be the climax of Elijah's ministry, and yet after he received a death threat from Queen Jezebel in the aftermath of this event, Elijah ran away until he arrived at this incredible low point in his life. Queen Jezebel had held close company with the prophets of Baal, and God's display of judgment against them was by extension a clear expression of wrath against her as well. In the course of this story are three keys to prevent or overcome burnout.

The first principle we see in the story of Elijah is the importance of remembering God's faithfulness in the past. One of the problems that contributed to Elijah's feeling of burnout was that he developed a short-term memory. God had just revealed His power in a miraculous way at Mount Carmel, and yet Elijah didn't think that God would continue to protect him against the very person that His power had just been displayed against.

God's faithfulness in the past should always serve as a reminder that He will continue to be faithful in the present and the future. Throughout the Bible, we see an importance placed on the act of remembering. On numerous occasions, God instructs the people of Israel to build a makeshift altar or pillar to serve as a reminder of what He had done and as a conversation starter to pass the story on to future generations. After the exile, First and Second Chronicles were written specifically to remind the people of how God had worked with the Israelites throughout their history. In the New Testament, Jesus left the practice of communion for the church as a means of remembering His sacrifice for our sins. We should not live in the past, but we should not forget it either. Failing to remember God's faithfulness causes us to worry needlessly and thus contributes to the sense of hopelessness that is often experienced during burnout.

The second factor we see in the story of Elijah is that he was in isolation. This is clear in 1 Kings 19:10 when he complains, *"I have been very zealous for the LORD God Almighty. The Israelites have rejected your covenant, torn down your altars, and put your prophets to death with the sword. I am the only one left, and now they are trying to kill me too.*"

This complaint echoes Elijah's proclamation back at Mount Carmel in 1 Kings 18:22: "*I am the only one of the LORD's prophets left, but Baal has four hundred and fifty prophets.*"

Whether Elijah was exaggerating or was actually the lone remaining prophet is not clear. When Elijah approaches the palace administrator Obadiah earlier in chapter 18 to set up the Mount Carmel showdown, Obadiah tells him, "*Haven't you heard, my lord, what I did while Jezebel was killing the prophets of the LORD? I hid a hundred of the LORD's prophets in two caves, fifty in each, and supplied them with food and water*" (1 Kings 18:13). The text does not indicate if Obadiah succeeded in saving these prophets or if they had eventually been captured and killed. Regardless, Elijah most definitely felt alone, and throughout the story he is in isolation.

One of the first observations that God makes about humanity is in Genesis 2:18: "*It is not good that the man should be alone*" (KJV). As part of the solution to his burnout, God instructs Elijah to anoint Elisha to become his understudy and ultimate successor following this event. For the remainder of Elijah's life, he worked in tandem with Elisha rather than alone.

Not only is it important to be part of a community in the form of the local church, but you should also have a select group of people who can serve as mentors, confidants, and accountability partners. You do not necessarily need to have regularly scheduled meetings with these people, but you should be able to identify a select few whom you can call if you need advice, prayer, support, or accountability. Proverbs 15:22 says, *Plans fail for lack of counsel, but with many advisers they succeed.* If you try to operate as a solo mission and don't have people who check in on you, you will probably burn yourself out.

The final observation we can make regarding burnout from

Elijah's cave experience is the way in which God ultimately revealed Himself to Elijah. In 1 Kings 19:11-13 we read:

> *Then a great and powerful wind tore the mountains apart and shattered the rocks before the LORD, but the LORD was not in the wind. After the wind there was an earthquake, but the LORD was not in the earthquake. After the earthquake came a fire, but the LORD was not in the fire. And after the fire came a gentle whisper. When Elijah heard it, he pulled his cloak over his face and went out and stood at the mouth of the cave.*

The first three manifestations that Elijah witnessed in which the presence of God was not found are all chaotic natural phenomena. One may have expected that God would have appeared in one of these three forms to show His great power, but on this occasion, God appeared as a gentle whisper. Elijah had known God's power at Mount Carmel, but now he needed to know God's peace. Psalm 46:10 commands us to know God in this way as well: *Be still, and know that I am God.* When you feel burned out, remove the clutter and the chaos from your mind and take some time to be still and rest in the reality of who God is. As 1 Peter 5:7 says, *Cast all your anxiety on him because he cares for you.* As long as you remain entrenched in the whirlwind of distractions that life provides, you will continue to remain in burnout mode. You need to take some time to be still and know that He is God, and then you can get back into ministry.

This last point is important. I'm a big baseball fan, and whenever a pitcher struggles, a coach often makes a mound visit. This does not always mean that a pitching change is coming. Many times the coach gives the pitcher an opportunity to regroup mentally, and then leaves him in the game to try to pitch through his slump. Just because you've hit a rough patch doesn't mean that you have to abandon the game. You may eventually conclude that God is calling you in a different direction, but you want to make that conclusion from a healthy mental state rather than a state of burnout. You might just need a chance to rest in God's presence, reorder some things in your life, and then get back in the game. This is how Elijah's time in the cave ends, as God commands him in verse 15 to *go back the way you came.* Don't let yourself become convinced that you have to live in your slump forever. You can overcome burnout and get back to a thriving ministry.

Conclusion

While it can be easy to become consumed in ministry, nothing you can do in ministry is as important as your personal relationship with God. Being a missionary does not make you exempt from spiritual droughts, and you will certainly find yourself in one sooner rather than later if you are not practicing spiritual disciplines. In contrast, if you are faithful to practice these disciplines and know how to address burnout when it comes, you will be positioned to have a thriving ministry for years to come.

Chapter 9

Final Logistical Preparations

When I came to my final weeks before moving overseas, I felt like there were a million last-minute preparations that I needed to make which I had not considered. I had been so focused on raising my support that I had failed to address all of the other important aspects of an international move. As a result, I spent my last week at home scrambling to get everything ready, rather than spending as much time as I would have liked with family and friends. This seems to be fairly common for new missionaries. In this final chapter, I will share some practical tips for things to consider as you prepare to move overseas.

Health Considerations

Healthcare systems around the world have significant differences. While the topic of health insurance was addressed in chapter 3, there are other considerations to be made besides how health insurance will be administered.

If you use prescription drugs on an ongoing basis for a chronic condition, you will need to discuss your international move with your doctor to decide your best course of action. While this may surprise you, in some parts of the world you can legally purchase most drugs from a pharmacy without a prescription from a doctor. If you are going to one of these countries and your condition is of the nature that your doctor can monitor it through video consultations, he or she may be able to continue as your primary physician and instruct you on what medications you should purchase and what doses you should take. Some doctors may not be willing to do this due to ethical or legal concerns, but others will not have a problem with it. If your doctor is unwilling to do this, or if your condition is of the nature that it cannot be monitored virtually, you will need to find a new doctor in whatever part of the world you are. No matter how well you think you know your condition and how easily accessible the medicine you need may be, it can be dangerous to self-medicate without the ongoing expertise of medical professionals who monitor your condition.

You should also note that in some parts of the world, medications arrive at the pharmacy prepackaged, and no actual mixing of drugs is done at the pharmacy. This means that the pharmacist may not have any significant training in pharmacology as you are accustomed to in the United States. If you ask the pharmacist for advice, without any formal medical knowledge, he or she will likely give you anecdotal opinions without medical facts.

Also, the drugs you purchase in foreign countries usually come from different laboratories than the medication you used in your home country. Such laboratories may not be subject to regulations of the Food and Drug Administration (FDA) or other oversight groups in your home country to ensure quality control of medications. This does not necessarily mean that a drug is unsafe to take, but it may have a slightly different chemical makeup even though it has the same name.

If you and your doctor determine that the medication you need is not available in the country to which you are moving or that the chemical differences are too great, you may need to wean off the medication you are using and begin a different medication with a similar function that is available in your destination country. This should be done before moving so your doctor can monitor the transition and insure that the new medication is working and not causing adverse side effects. If this is not an option and the medication is vital, you may need to consider planned trips back home to refill prescriptions in the largest allowable quantity or choose a different country than you had originally planned.

No missionary wants to hear this, but if your condition is severe, it may need to be considered. Most doctors do not treat soon-to-be expats, so your doctor may not have the answers you need regarding the availability or strength of medications in your new destination country. While he or she can certainly research this, you may also ask your local contacts through your organization to visit a few local pharmacies to check on the availability of the medication you will need. You might also consult a travel doctor who may have more knowledge of international health matters than the average general doctor.

A second concern that should be considered by anyone moving overseas is the need for additional vaccinations for diseases that you do not encounter at home. Some countries require travelers to show proof that they have received certain vaccinations before entering the country. Even if the country doesn't require it, you would be wise to get any recommended vaccinations before moving.

Not all mission organizations make it a priority to inform their missionaries of vaccine recommendations, but you can find a list of recommended vaccines by country of travel on the Centers for Disease Control (CDC) website. A travel doctor can administer these vaccines, but they may not be covered by your health insurance if the disease is not common in your home country. If this is the case, or if you come from a country where the cost of healthcare is inflated, you might consider getting the vaccination upon your arrival in the country of your destination. If you do decide to get the vaccination in your home country, keep in mind that many vaccines require multiple rounds of injection, so start the process soon enough to finish all of them before you leave.

Although some vaccines may seem unnecessary or a nuisance, I recommend getting all of the vaccinations that the CDC recommends for your country. Before I moved to El Salvador, I wrestled with whether or not to get a rabies vaccination. Although it was recommended by the CDC, it was expensive, and I had never been bit by a dog before in my life. Plus, even if I got bit, I reasoned that rabies prevention requires a post-bite vaccination anyway. When combined with the administration of human rabies immune globulin (HRIG), post-bite vaccinations are effective at preventing the disease if treatment is started immediately. After I consulted with someone who had worked in public health with the Peace Corps and discovered through research that the HRIG for post-bite rabies prevention treatment was in scarce supply in El Salvador, I decided it was best to play it safe and get the vaccination.

This ended up being the right decision. During my first year in El Salvador, I camped in a remote location that we had hiked to where I was bitten by an unprovoked stray dog. The bite was not severe, but it pierced the skin and required a hospital visit. After talking with others, it turned out that many people in El Salvador have been bitten by a stray dog at some point in their lives, so it was probably just a matter of time before this happened to me.

It took a while to get to the hospital because we were so far from the city, and when I arrived, I could see the visible concern on the doctor's face. When I showed him my vaccination record that indicated I had already been vaccinated preventively for rabies, he was relieved. Since I already had antibodies in my system, all I needed was two booster shots, and there was no problem whatsoever. Had I not received the rabies vaccination beforehand, the situation would have been more complicated. The moral of this story is that even if you don't think you need a vaccination, it's best to follow the recommendations.

A final health concern for missionaries is how much they should expose their bodies to local food and water from sources that could be contaminated. Street food or food purchased in the market of developing countries has been subjected to much lower hygiene standards than what Westerners are accustomed to. Tap water similarly can contain bacteria and parasites that can make you sick. The typical mission trip always includes at least one person who gets sick, and when you move overseas, you will probably get sick at some point as well. This happened to me in my sixth month in El Salvador, and I didn't eat a full meal for four consecutive days and had to take parasite medication.

Two opposite extremes emerge when it comes to the topic of food and water consumption. The first is to listen to all recommendations, which basically means never eating anything that wasn't bought in a grocery store and never drinking anything if you don't know where the water came from. The other extreme is to throw yourself full force into eating and drinking from unhygienic sources as much as possible to try to force your body to adjust to the new bacteria and parasites. This may sound crazy, but some missionaries have committed to drinking only tap water in their homes even though it may not be clean. The irony of this is that many locals don't even do this.

My preference is somewhere between the two extremes. When I am at home, I buy most of my food from the grocery store and only drink filtered water. However, when I am out and about, I eat wherever the group wants to eat, and if I am in someone's home, I eat and drink what is served to me without asking questions. At some ministry sites, I can almost guarantee that the food being served includes unfiltered water and meat that has been sitting out in the market with limited refrigeration, but it would be impossible to minister amongst average Salvadorans and avoid this entirely.

I'd recommend that when you are on your own time, be mindful of what you eat and drink, especially in the beginning of your time overseas. However, when you are doing ministry or are with others, I'd recommend not raising objections to what is available. Be smart about drinking bottled water if it's available, but if someone from a humble background serves a bowl of soup, I don't ask if the water was filtered. Doing this would be offensive. Also, I don't avoid situations where something like this might happen. Doing so would greatly hamper the ability to minister in person.

When you need to see a doctor, as you undoubtedly will at some point during your time overseas, remember that the U.S. embassy in most countries has a list online of doctors they recommend who are highly trained and who often speak English. Whether or not you are from the United States, there is nothing preventing you from using the list that all U.S. embassies provide publicly on their websites.

Taxes

Some missionaries assume that when they move overseas, they no longer have any tax liability in their home country. I cannot speak for all countries, but in the United States this is definitely not true. As a U.S. citizen, you will still be required to pay FICA or SECA taxes, depending on how your employment is classified. (Technically, there are limited ways to get exemptions to this for some religious workers, but it is not the norm and is a more technical area of the tax code than I am qualified to discuss.) You will also be subject to the same tax-filing requirements as any other U.S. citizen at home and may have to file a state income tax return as well.

Although you must file a tax return, you may be able to avoid paying U.S. income tax by using the Foreign Earned Income Exemption. This exemption allows U.S. citizens to exempt any earned income they make while overseas, even if that income comes from a U.S. source. If they have met a particular minimum number of days spent overseas within the period of a year, or they are considered bona fide residents of a foreign country, they qualify for that exemption. There are limits to how much income can be exempted annually, but these limits are well above what the average missionary makes. If you are not from the United States, you should research any exemptions from your home country.

If this is making your head spin, you're not alone. Taxes can be confusing enough already, and adding the element of being overseas only makes it more difficult. It is so confusing that I have talked to different CPAs about tax liability questions and have received different answers. I'd recommend that you budget the assistance of an expat tax-preparation service to file your tax returns. Even though this will cost much more than what you're accustomed to paying at home, it is the best way to ensure that your taxes are filed properly and that you do not run into problems. Even if you previously filed your own taxes, I recommend hiring a professional to do them your first year. Then you can use that tax return as a model to file in future years if you are confident that you understand the process. I had filed my own taxes before moving overseas, and I found that filing taxes as an expat is infinitely more confusing and intricate than filing taxes were before.

Lastly, you need to consult an immigration lawyer and/or a tax accountant in the country to which you will be moving to determine if you will be required to pay income taxes in your new country of residence. Some countries have residency categories and visa types that do not require an immigrant to pay local income taxes if they receive their income through a foreign source. In other countries, you could be required to pay local income tax. It would be impossible to divulge all of the possible information you will need regarding taxes here, and tax codes will undoubtedly change following this book's release. The important thing is that you are aware of your potential tax liabilities and are in contact with knowledgeable professionals to ensure that you fulfill your legal requirements both at home and abroad.

Banking

Before you move overseas, you will probably want to switch banks. Most banks charge foreign transaction fees, which will not be compatible for you if you are living overseas. In addition to finding a bank that doesn't have foreign transaction fees, you will want to find a bank that does not charge ATM fees for using the ATMs of other financial institutions, because banks in your home country will likely not have their own ATMs in the country where you are. Even better, find a bank that will rebate you for fees charged by the ATM owner. This may sound too good to be true, but as of the writing of this book, I know of at least one bank (Schwab) that has this policy. A quick search online of the best banks for expats should turn up enough information to help you choose the best bank for yourself.

Some missionaries never open a bank account overseas but

rather continue to use their bank from back home. Others find that paying bills or making large cash withdrawals is more convenient with a local bank account. Whether or not you choose to do this is up to you, but you should be aware that the requirements for immigrants to open a bank account can be more cumbersome than for local citizens in some parts of the world. Also, having a foreign bank account may carry tax-reporting requirements back home, depending on how much money you have had in the account.

Lastly, if you are going to a region that has a history of instability, it may not be wise to use a local bank account as your main account. If the situation gets hostile or dangerous in the country where you are and you have to leave unexpectedly, you may lose any money that you had in your foreign bank account.

Legal Documents

You will need legal documents from home during your time overseas, both for immigration purposes and for a slew of other reasons. Before you leave, you should confirm what documents you will need to present for immigration purposes and get these in order ahead of time. I can assure you from experience that it is much more difficult to acquire such documents while abroad. If you are required to present a background check, be sure to get the correct type that is requested, as there are various types of background checks. You should also bring any other important legal documents for which a need may eventually arise during your time abroad, such as a marriage certificate, a birth certificate, or a driver's license. It is important to note, though, that legal documents will generally not be recognized in a foreign country unless they are apostilled.

An apostille is a form of notarization for international purposes, established as a means to ensure document authenticity at an international summit called the Hague Convention. The vast majority of countries are part of the agreement that resulted from this convention, and assuming that both your home country and your destination country were part of the agreement, you will need to get apostilled copies of all of your legal documents before leaving. Apostilles are issued by federal, state, and local governments rather than private parties. You will need to consult with the branch of government that issued a particular document to determine how to get that document apostilled. You will want to start this process early with plenty of time to spare before leaving the country, because it is not as simple as showing up with all of your documents to get them stamped in one session. If you happen to be from, or are going to, one of the rare countries that was not part of the Hague Convention, you will need to research what the requirements are in your situation for legal documents to be accepted.

Schooling

If you have children, navigating the change in schools during an international move can be challenging. My knowledge is limited here since I do not yet have children, but I know that not all countries follow the same academic calendar. If your home country and your destination country do not share the same school year, and you do not plan to homeschool, you will need to determine the best means of making the transition. One option is to leave in the middle of the school year to start at the onset of a new school year in your destination country. Another option is to leave at the end of the school year and jump into the middle of the school year in your destination country. A third option, which most missionaries that I know seem to choose, is to send your children to an international school that follows the school year of your home country rather than the standard school year of your destination country. Such schools are generally found only in large metropolitan areas, though, so if your ministry is located outside of such an area, you may have a long commute if you choose this option.

STEP

If you are a U.S. citizen or national, you should enroll in the Smart Traveler Enrollment Program (STEP) before leaving the country. STEP is a free service that allows the Department of State (or State Department) to have your contact information and general whereabouts. Once enrolled, you will receive emails from the State Department whenever important information arises concerning the state of the country that you should be aware of. In the event of an emergency, the Department of State will also use the STEP database to locate, contact, and evacuate U.S. citizens and nationals. I would assume that most countries have a similar service that you can research if you are from a country other than the United States.

Address Problems

When missionaries leave their home country to go overseas for long-term ministry assignments, they often sell their home or give up the place that they had been renting. This can cause some unwanted complications, because banks and other institutions back home, with whom a person may need to maintain business, will often require you to have a local address on file. Many people resolve this by using the address of a family member, but if this is not possible in your situation, you can rent what's known as a virtual address. I do not know if this is available in all countries, but it is available in the United States. A virtual address is essentially a P.O. Box that doesn't actually exist. It will appear as a U.S. address, but the company managing the address will forward all mail to your address overseas. Virtual addresses have a monthly fee, and international mailings are not reliable in all parts of the world, which makes this a less ideal option than using the address of a family member. However, if you are stuck, you may want to explore this option. Similar services also exist to give you a phone number from back home that will forward calls to your cell phone while you have a foreign cell-phone number if this is important to you.

Passport Renewal

While not commonly known, you should be aware as a missionary that some countries restrict travel if your passport is within six months of expiration. I've never really understood the logic behind this, as it defeats the purpose of the expiration date. However, the point to realize is that you should never allow your passport to come within six months of expiring. Depending on the date on your passport and its life span, you may not have to worry about it for many years. However, it is something that you should keep in mind as the need arises. If you are overseas when your passport needs renewal, most countries have passport renewal services available at their embassies.

Conclusion

I hope you have found this book to be helpful in your journey to become a missionary. You may feel relieved to have a better understanding of the process, or you may feel overwhelmed by how many components there are. Regardless of how you feel, though, I can guarantee that God has great plans for your life that He will fulfill in His timing if you seek Him with all your heart. I don't know where you are on your journey, but I would like to end this book by praying for you.

God,
Thank you so much for giving me the opportunity to
write this book. I pray that you will have your hand
upon the person reading this in a powerful way.
Mold them into a greater reflection of Jesus and
fill them with your heart. Give them a clear under-
standing of the call you have on their lives, and
give them a fresh passion for that calling. Fill them
with the Holy Spirit and renew their fervor day by
day. Regardless of the direction that their lives take,
whether into vocational mission work or something
entirely different, I pray that you will use them to
build your kingdom in the context where you have
placed them. Most importantly, I pray that they
will know and internalize how great your love is for
them.
In the name of Jesus,
Amen.

Acknowledgements

Thank you to my parents, grandparents, sister, and extended family for believing in me and supporting me in my mission endeavors. Many people would not be as supportive of their son, grandson, or brother living and working in a developing country far from home. Thank you, Mom, for suggesting that I write this book. Thank you Pastors Don Brasco, Brent Galbreath, Mike Cooper, and Andrew Gard for shaping my walk with God in the years that I sat under your leadership. Thank you Pastor

Mike Cooper (different person, same name) and Steve Hill for giving me the opportunity to serve at the Dream Center and for showing me what it means to live with a mission mindset.

Thank you to my professors at Southeastern University who not only taught me but also discipled me and framed my understanding of ministry. Thank you especially, Professor Jason Old, for fostering my interest in Latin America and giving me my first opportunity to visit Central America.

Thank you, Dave Greco, for answering my many questions about missions. Thank you to all of my friends back home who are too many to mention but who have enriched my walk with God. Thank you to Christ For the City for the opportunity to do full-time foreign mission work and to all the financial donors and prayer warriors who have provided support for both the ministry and me.

Thank you to everyone who took me under their wing when I arrived in El Salvador: Barbara Rowe, Jake Hjemvick, Karen Mejia, Joel Henrriquez, and many more. Thank you to all my local Salvadoran friends who accepted me as one of their own. Thank you to the inmates of Tonacatepeque for making the ministry worthwhile.

Thank you Jeremiah Zeiset and Aneko Press for believing in this book and giving me the opportunity to publish it.

And most importantly, thank you, Lord, first for redeeming me and then for calling me into such an awesome ministry.

Recommended Reading

Corbett, Steve, and Brian Fikkert. *When Helping Hurts: How to Alleviate Poverty Without Hurting the Poor and Yourself.* Chicago: Moody Publishers, 2014.

Hofstede, Geert, Gert Jan Hofstede, and Michael Minkov. *Cultures and Organizations: Software of the Mind.* 3rd ed. New York: McGraw-Hill, 2010.

Kraft, Charles H. *Communication Theory for Christian Witness.* Maryknoll, NY: Orbis Books, 1997.

Lingenfelter, Sherwood G., and Marvin K. Mayers. *Ministering Cross-Culturally.* 2nd ed. Grand Rapids: Baker Academic, 2003.

Piper, John. *Don't Waste Your Life.* Wheaton, IL: Crossway Books, 2018.

Shadrach, Steve, and Scott Morton. *The God Ask.* Fayetteville, AR: CMM Press, 2013.

Sider Ronald J. *Good News and Good Works: A Theology for the Whole Gospel.* Grand Rapids, MI: Baker Books, 1999.

Stanley, Andy, Reggie Joiner, and Lane Jones. *7 Practices of Effective Ministry.* Multnomah Books, 2004.

Steffen, Tom A., and Lois McKinney Douglas. *Encountering Missionary Life and Work: Preparing for Intercultural Ministry.* Grand Rapids, MI: Baker Academic, 2008.

About the Author

Danny Lamastra holds an MA in Ministerial Leadership and an MBA from Southeastern University. He has been on staff at Southeastern University in Lakeland, Florida, and Esperanza College of Eastern University in Philadelphia, Pennsylvania. After sensing God's call to full-time missionary service, Danny moved to El Salvador in 2018 to begin working with Christ For the City International. During his time there, he has served primarily in a prison ministry for convicted gang members.

Connect with Danny:
cfci.org/dannylamastra
dannylamastra@gmail.com

Made in the USA
Las Vegas, NV
19 February 2022

44228713R00085